WAY

**DO NOT REMOVE
CARDS FROM POCKET**

The Penny Whistle™

ANY DAY IS A HOLIDAY PARTY BOOK

by Meredith Brokaw
& Annie Gilbar

DESIGNED & ILLUSTRATED
BY JILL WEBER

A FIRESIDE BOOK PUBLISHED BY SIMON & SCHUSTER

F

F I R E S I D E
Rockefeller Center
1230 Avenue of the Americas
New York, NY 10020

FIRESIDE and colophon are registered trademarks of Simon & Schuster Inc.

Designed by Jill Weber

Manufactured in the United States of America

10 9 8 7 6 5 4 3 2 1

Library of Congress Cataloging-in-Publication Data

Brokaw, Meredith.
     The Penny Whistle any day is a holiday party book / by Meredith
Brokaw & Annie Gilbar ; designed & illustrated by Jill Weber.
          p.   cm.
     "A Fireside book".
     On t.p. the registered trademark symbol "TM" is superscript
following "whistle" in the title.
     Includes index.
     1. Children's parties.   2. Entertaining.   I. Gilbar, Annie.
II. Weber, Jill.   III. Title.
GV1205.B656   1996
793.2 ' 1--dc20   96-15083
                                                                         CIP

ISBN 0-684-83192-9
     0-684-80917-6 (pbk.)

To Creative
Party Planners
Everywhere

The Penny Whistle Party Planner

The Penny Whistle Lunch Box Book

The Penny Whistle Halloween Book

The Penny Whistle Christmas Party Book

The Penny Whistle Birthday Party Book

The Penny Whistle Sick-in-Bed Book

The Penny Whistle Traveling with Kids Book

ACKNOWLEDGMENTS

 First and foremost, thank you to the Brokaws, the Gilbars,
and the Webers, extended families all.

Thanks to our longtime and steadfast editor, Sydney Miner.
And to all the friends, oldtimers and new ones, readers included,
for your anecdotes and tips that are throughout the book.
Your stories are wonderful, and your memories are better than ours!

Peggy and Whitney Ackerman
Vivian, Alex, and Wynne Auld
Nadine, Emily, Avi, and Lynne Barbasch
Lee Berber
Cammy Blackstone
Sandra and Alex Brown
Amos Buhai
Joanie Donohue
Cynthia Dougherty

Carole Ference
Jane, Robert, and Rachael Greenberg
Aaron Greenberg
Robert Gunther
Lindsay, Erica, and Perry Heard
Anne Hobbs
Karen, Michelle, and Christopher Hogan
The Inglis Family
The Israel Family
Geri Jansen
Brook Joseph
Isabel and Jamie Kaplan
Mike Klecan
Jeremy Konner
Diane Koge-Anders

Wanda Lau
Benjamin and Norman Lear
Cara, Jake, and Adam Levine
Beverly Maxwell
The Mintz Family
Mary Murphy and Megen Swertlow
Nancy Neisinger
The Niles Family
The O'Halloran Family
Jane Paley
Hilda and Michael Petruncola
Joey and Mary Catherine Quinn
Beverly Riehm and family
The Root Family
Susan Russell
Sam and Jake Sadle
Lisa Simpson
Amis Stevens
Brenda and Sally Sure
Janice Gilbar Treadwell
Leslie Ward
The Wyler Family
Beth Yow

Contents

Introduction

ANY DAY CAN BE A HOLIDAY. Christmas, Thanksgiving, Passover, Mother's Day—those holidays are familiar, and we are used to observing them. But many other days lend themselves to celebrations. Birthdays and anniversaries come around only once a year, but there are plenty of "little occasions" that call for attention. By marking a special day, whether serious or silly, you'll make the occasion even more memorable and give it extra meaning.

The day the new baby comes home from the hospital, the braces come off, the driver's license is finally in your child's hand, or school lets out for the summer—all qualify as opportunities for celebration. Sharing such personal and distinctive occasions, each of which can hold a special place in your life, is what *The Penny Whistle Any Day Is a Holiday Party Book* is all about.

Personal occasions or "holidays" are as varied as the friends who celebrate them. When Remy Weber was in kindergarten, his teacher left to have a baby. The Webers decided to organize a quilt-making party so the kids in the class could celebrate and commemorate this special occasion in their teacher's life. Jill gave each child in the class a white square of cotton fabric and fabric crayons. She then took each signed drawing, ironed the artwork in to make it permanent, and sewed it to a backing. The

★ *When a last-minute ticket to the musical* Annie *became available, Perry Heard took her ten-year-old daughter, Lindsay. It was a great way to celebrate being red-haired and freckle-faced.*

result was a beautiful gift and a party that everyone enjoyed and remembered.

The Heard family, who live in Maine, celebrated the day their new puppy came home from the ASPCA. They went to the park for a romp; stopped by the pet store for food, collar, leash, and toys; and had a Dog Name discussion for hours. They all played games with the new puppy, took pictures of everyone romping around, and had a great time.

For Lisa Gilbar's graduation, the Gilbars invited a group of the other graduates and some adult friends for a pool party. After the formal cap-and-gown ceremony, the kids couldn't wait to ditch the gowns, put on their swimsuits, and jump in the pool, while the adults relished seeing these "nearly adults" acting like kids again.

Cynthia Dougherty's family (all boys, aged 18, 15, 6, and 2) have an informal agreement: any day when the temperature is forecast to be 103 degrees or more, they get to celebrate Upside Down Day. Pillows go to the bottoms of the beds; dinner is served in the morning and breakfast at night. Of course, the dessert comes first, followed by the appetizers. If they go swimming, they must dive in backward.

Brook Joseph came across her two children, aged 7 and 8, poring over the kitchen calendar one day. When asked what they were doing, they replied, "We're planning our Open Space Party." "What's that?" Brook asked. "See all these open spaces on the calendar after Valentine's Day and before the Fourth of July? We want to fill one up with a party." And they did.

Having a two-hour Camp Runamok party on a summer day (see page 26) is a piece of cake compared with the party Meredith gave for nine of her nieces and nephews. While Meredith and her brothers and sisters were having a family reunion, Meredith decided that the kids needed their own celebration, so her version of our Camp Runamok party was a five-day marathon party on a ranch in Montana. The Brokaws put up a big ten- by twelve-foot wall tent in the yard; took their kids on nature hikes; taught them how to press wildflowers, make lanyard key rings, paint rocks, and make sand art; had neighborhood teenagers teach the kids how to perform some barn chores; and provided lots of other activities. The kids also learned how to ride. Every night, they all sat around a campfire and the kids took turns telling ghost stories and sang their favorite camp songs. Everyone gorged on s'mores every night!

Throughout, guests took turns taking pictures of the daily festivities (which the Brokaws sent to the kids so they'd have ready-made memories of their own), and Meredith made one large scrapbook that the kids could look at on their return. The "camp" for the kids turned out to be a celebration that they will remember forever.

★ *Professional tennis player Anne Hobbs spent much of her youth traveling throughout England on the tennis circuit. She remembers the looming sight of the Ferris wheel at a carnival on the outskirts of a small town and the fun that unexpectedly occurred for her and the family. It was the best holiday of all.*

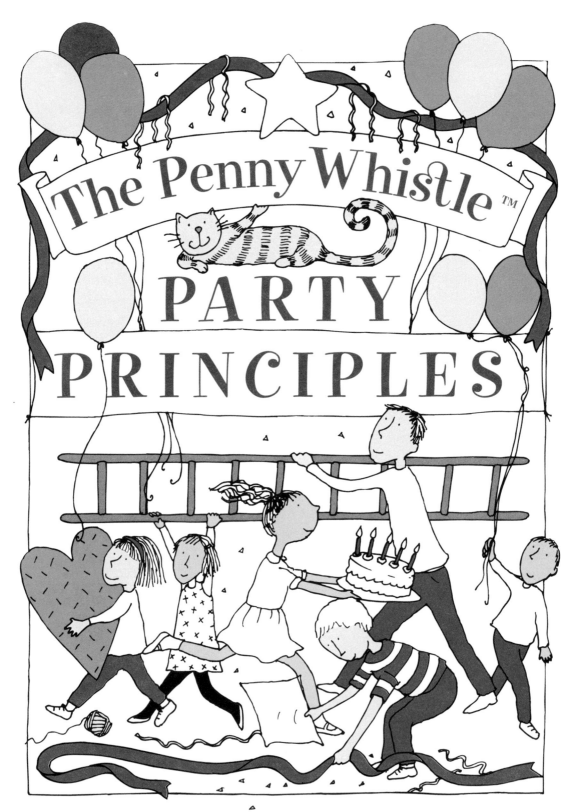

The Penny Whistle™ PARTY PRINCIPLES

YOU WON'T BE SORRY

It's worthwhile to take the time to celebrate together, especially if the holiday is a unique part of your family's life. Children always look forward to parties, and when the party focuses on them and their accomplishments and experiences, the occasion has much more meaning. Take the time. You won't be sorry!

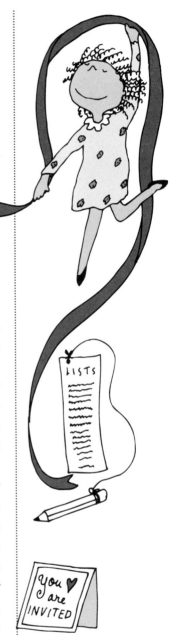

PLANNING FOR SPECIAL EVENTS

Let the reason for the party carry the day. If you allow the central idea to influence everything you do, from sending the invitations to organizing activities, decorations, and food, you will greatly simplify the process of putting together a party. Our plans do half the work for you. You'll find that your own imagination and creativity will be sparked by reading our suggestions and by checking the anecdotes and tips from our many friends and readers.

Often, your celebration will be primarily for your family members. Let them plan the party with you. Not only will this lighten the workload, but the occasion itself can be even more memorable for all the participants. This is a good time to include relatives and friends in the planning process. If you are giving a party to commemorate Grandparents' Day, ask other relatives to bring their own pictures of Grandma and Grandpa, relate anecdotes, or contribute an heirloom recipe. If you are cheering your child's graduation, dig into the attic to uncover some childhood toys and photographs—and be sure to ask friends and aunts and uncles to bring their mementos as well. If this is the day your child finally gets rid of those braces, ask friends to bring pictures of themselves in their braces.

DO IT YOURSELF

This is your party, and it should be uniquely and personally yours. Anyone can hire a party planner to "do" a party. There is nothing personal about it, and other parties will be just like yours. But most important, by delegating the creation of your party to an outsider you will miss a great opportunity for your children to share a special experience together. Much of the work in party giving is in the planning and organizing—but by following our guidelines and step-by-step party ideas, the "workload" turns into "pleasure planning" that everyone can share.

PLAN THE PARTY TOGETHER

Involving the whole family in the party planning is important to the success of the event. Every member of your family will have more fun at the party if all are involved in the planning process, and the entire procedure will be more pleasurable and more effectively organized for you. Just remember:

★ Listen to others' ideas and requests.

★ Include as many people as possible in the planning process.

★ Assign responsibilities and tasks to others, to give everyone a sense of involvement and participation and to make life easier for you.

★ Share in making choices; give members of your immediate family the chance to take part in the decision-making process concerning invitations, themes, decorations, and

★ *Perry Heard likes celebrating nonholidays simply because there are no expectations for perfection, and she finds that spontaneity and unexpected events are more fun for everyone.*

TEMPER YOUR EXPECTATIONS

Try not to get carried away with planning the party. This is only a party, not an international summit conference. Put the process and event into perspective, and your tensions and worries about its success will diminish. If the unexpected happens, you will handle it. If a game or an activity is a bust, you'll have another at your fingertips. If one guest is not having a good time, others are. Remember—guests expect to have a good time. You don't need total perfection to have a successful party. Take the pressure off yourself by remembering that it's just a party, and everyone *will* have fun.

★ *San Franciscans Sandra Brown and daughter Alex established a penalty jar years ago. Each had to contribute (25 cents for mom and 5 cents for daughter) whenever there was a slight misunderstanding (or worse!). Whenever the Penalty Jar had accumulated enough money, they used the "fines" for a dinner out to celebrate their togetherness.*

PLAN FOR EVERY MOMENT

All our party plans stress the point that planning a party is like constructing a play: you need a beginning, a middle, and an end. When all the guests are children, you need to ensure there are activities to keep them occupied at all times. A family party has a somewhat different rhythm; it is successful when there are activities or projects for a variety of people to do at different times.

ACT ONE ★

Make sure that all incoming guests feel welcome. Organize an activity or ask for help with a last-minute chore. Designate places for your guests to congregate. This is the time to bring old friends together or introduce new guests to each other.

★ *A Seattle mom, Nancy Neisinger, interested in diverting her kids from playing war games, came up with "Onstage" parties, held either outside or anywhere in the house. The prop boxes that she adds to regularly serve as the focus for the actors in their impromptu theater performances. She helps the kids pick a theme for the play of the day but encourages them to make the rules, select the roles, and write the script.*

ACT TWO ★

The party. All the activities, games, projects, and food service take place during this phase.

ACT THREE—THE FINALE ★

As the party winds down, quieter activities should be planned. This is the time for quiet games, for conversation, and for passing out favors. Sometimes you can even begin cleaning up; it can make guests feel like part of the family.

EXPRESS YOURSELF

Parties should reflect the individuality of the giver. You will find this book full of hints and suggestions that will also trigger your own imagination to create a party that is all yours.

YOUR PARTY IS A CELEBRATION, NOT A COMPETITION

Keep in mind what your celebration is really about. Don't overdo; spending a lot of money does not make a party a success and may send the wrong message to your children that money buys success and ensures a good time. Lavish extravaganzas can make people feel uncomfortable and are most often inappropriate to the occasion.

Always keep in mind that really successful parties do not need to be expensive. That's why you will find suggested items you can buy or make according to your time and budget. These parties are for your children and your family. They need not make headlines or set any records. We believe in the creative, casual approach: a party should be fun while it is happening and result in happy memories.

ENCOURAGE PARTICIPATION

Don't overload yourself with so many last-minute tasks that you don't get to participate in and enjoy the festivities. Your active involvement in the party means getting help. Consider asking others to bring food or assist with the preparations. Relatives, friends, and even the kids are often more than willing to help out if given the chance. They'll feel as if their assistance is crucial to the success of the party (and it is!).

PLAN AHEAD

That's our middle name. Give yourself enough time to plan the party. Preparing ahead of time for all the things you will need takes the guesswork and worry out of a party. Follow our guidelines—make those lists, buy the ingredients ahead of time, delegate tasks, and organize, organize, organize—and everything will fall easily into place.

BE FLEXIBLE

One of the best things about the many Penny Whistle parties is that they afford you as much flexibility as you want and need. We have designed and organized complete parties, but many of their parts are interchangeable. If you are planning the Friday the 13th party but can't wait to play one of the games in the Stampede party—do it! The same is true of our suggestions for menus and activities. It is our hope that the ideas you read about here will inspire your own creative impulses.

TAKE PICTURES

Take *lots* of pictures. Everyone will want to remember the party. Assign the job of photographer to a family member or close friend. You can also buy several disposable cameras and give them out to people at the party. Remember to begin at the beginning; you don't want to start taking pictures when the party is half over! Use your own video camera or borrow or rent one, and play the tape back at the end of the party. It's amazing how much everyone likes to see himself on the screen! Instant photographs make wonderful party favors. If you are using 35 mm film, you may want to duplicate special photographs of the guests and send them to everyone after the party.

Above all, HAVE FUN!

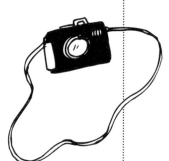

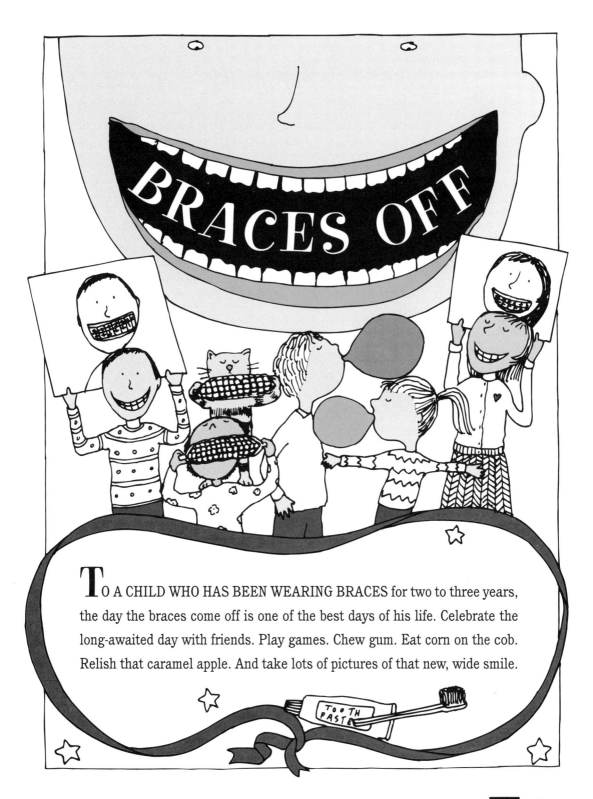

BRACES OFF

To A CHILD WHO HAS BEEN WEARING BRACES for two to three years, the day the braces come off is one of the best days of his life. Celebrate the long-awaited day with friends. Play games. Chew gum. Eat corn on the cob. Relish that caramel apple. And take lots of pictures of that new, wide smile.

INVITATION

Cut a lip-shaped invitation from white oak tag or heavy construction paper. Cut a horizontal slit as the mouth opening, and attach fasteners to the lower side to look like braces. Color the lips red.

BACK

BRACES OFF
PARTY

WIRE FASTENER

CUT SLIT

PARTY AT JULIE FOSTER'S

333 PINE ST. SAT, OCT. 12TH

8-10 PM R.S.V.P. 567-1234

F R O N T

DECORATIONS

If they are available, use your child's old x-rays, plaster molds from the orthodontist, and even that worn-out retainer as props for the party. You can photocopy the x-rays in different colors and hang them around the room. Otherwise, look for fake teeth at novelty stores to use as table decorations—wacky toothbrushes, flavored toothpaste, wax lips, vamp fangs, sample-size bottles of mouthwash. These can also be given out as favors after the party.

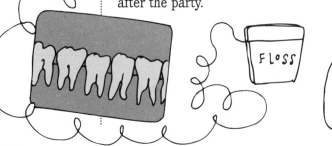

FLOSS

MOUTH WASH

ACTIVITIES

X-RAYS

Make photocopies of a set of x-rays of your child's teeth. They'll be in black and white. Hand out colored markers to all the guests so they can color them in and create very abstract art. Lisa's friends did this and couldn't believe the variety of designs that the different colors could make. You can also glue glitter and sequins to the "paintings."

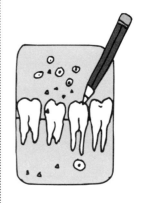

MOUTHING OFF

As guests arrive at the party, take close-up instant photos of their mouths. Later in the party, have guests try to identify each other by their smiles.

MOLARS VS. WISDOM TEETH

Guests are divided into two teams—the Molars and the Wisdom Teeth—who search for a bubble gum treasure. Write clues that lead the guests from one place to another to find the following items (or come up with your own):

a lipstick print

MY "SMACKS" WON'T HURT YOU— THEY'LL SMOOCH You!

a shoe with its tongue hanging out

THIS DOG WON'T NEED AN APPLE, BUT MAYBE A SNAPPLE!

dental floss

I GLIDE THROUGH YOUR PEARLS WITH THE GREATEST OF EASE

an apple with a bite taken out of it

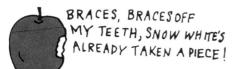

BRACES, BRACES OFF MY TEETH, SNOW WHITE'S ALREADY TAKEN A PIECE!

a toothbrush

I CAN'T GET OUT THE TANGLES, BUT I CAN REACH ALL THE ANGLES!

a mini-tube of toothpaste

"AIM™" FOR MY "CREST™"

23

A SWEET STORY

This is a variation on one of our favorite games from the Club Casino party in *The Penny Whistle Birthday Party Book*. Collect as many different kinds of candy as you can; their names are used as inspiration for a fill-in-the-blanks game. On a large foam board with a thick black marker, write out the following story or make up one of your own. Place all the candy on a nearby table. The names of the candies are used to fill in the blanks. The game can be hilarious, as the blanks are filled in with some outlandish choices: Mars, Milky Way, Life Savers, Nerds, Hot Tamales, Runts, Charms, Milk Duds, Charleston Chew, Snow Caps, Mr. Goodbar, Trident, Bubble Yum, Double Bubble, Sugar Babies.

Traveling at light speed through the _____, our favorite alien _____, otherwise known as _____, was racing against the clock. Seems a warring gang, _____, threatened to turn the entire universe into _____, and it was up the magical _____ powers to get things straight. As her spaceship zoomed through the ozone layer made of _____ the throttle suddenly sounded a "BOOM" and fell quickly through the air. "AHHHHHH—I'm going to hit the land of _____ and I'll miss saving the universe." Luckily, another armed force, _____, had spies surveying the scene and intervened with their ships. Together they rushed toward the battle site. Would they save the day? Tune in next time.

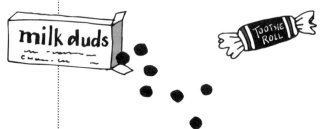

CANDY WHEELS

These are beautiful creations that are fun to make and then to eat. At a large candy store that sells candy by the pound or in large bags, buy assorted candies in all shapes, colors, and sizes. The jellied kind are particularly attractive. You also need the largest paper plates you can find, or cardboard cut into 12- to 18-inch circles for big wheels that can be displayed and eaten at the end of the party, or 8-inch paper plates for an individual wheel that can be wrapped with plastic wrap and taken home.

Each guest creates a mosaic design with the candy.

FAVORS

Bags of gum

Chewy candy

Chattering teeth (wind-ups)

Toothbrushes and toothpaste

Lipstick case with mirror

Flavored dental floss

★ *When Wanda Lau got her braces off, her friends gave her baskets of gifts like sticky candies, Polident, denture-washing accessories, gum, a caramel apple—and she ate them all (except the denture stuff, which she kept just to remind her of that special day).*

MENU

MEAT LOAF BURGERS

CORN ON THE COB

CARAMEL APPLES

CANDY WHEELS (see above)

CAMP RUNAMOK

$\mathbf{S}$UMMERTIME—WHEN ANY DAY *IS* A HOLIDAY—is the right time to set up a mini-camp party for a bunch of friends. Peggy Ackerman, from Pasadena, California, developed Camp Runamok for her son Whitney's sixth birthday (but you don't need a birthday as an excuse to give this party). Her delightful creativity and careful planning made the party a great hit, and your party will be a cinch to do as well with these party plans. This type of theme is perfect as is for six- to eight-year-olds, but it can be modified to work for younger or older kids.

INVITATION

These invitations were created using a computer for the text and a rubber-stamp illustration on the front. Whitney colored in the picture, stuffed the envelopes, and added some camp-theme stickers on the outside.

Have the invitations printed on 8½- by 11-inch colored paper and fold them in fourths. Put information about time, date, place, and phone number for RSVP on the left; if you're inspired, compose a short poem setting a camp theme on the right. You can modify or eliminate the poem if you choose. The Ackermans' rhyme started like this:

ribit

FOR: WHITNEY ACKERMAN
DATE: JUNE 20
RSVP 567-1234

FROGS IN YOUR POCKET, SAND IN YOUR SHOES! FRECKLES ON YOUR FACE, BIRTHDAY NEWS!

YES, THAT'S RIGHT - A PARTY IS PLANNED - JUNE 20 IS THE DATE - BE THERE IF YOU CAN

come to CAMP RUNAMOK

DECORATIONS

T-shirts shout "CAMP." Buy inexpensive white shirts and, using fabric paint, stencil the backs with your child's favorite animal shape. If you have the time (and patience), CAMP RUNAMOK stenciled on the front would be a hit. As soon as the guests arrive, give out the shirts for everyone to wear during the party.

ACTIVITIES

The party should have the organized feeling of a day camp, with a timetable for the activities of the day. You might even write out the schedule on a chalk board to keep everything moving. Use our "camp clock," or create an activity list that will work for you.

6:00 Parents who have volunteered to help arrive.

6:30 Children start arriving and are given a T-shirt to change into. Start the orientation tour of the "Camp Facilities," using the first to arrive as guides for the newer arrivals. Point out the Mess Hall, Craft Nook, Fishing Hole, and Playground.

6:45 Camp photo.

7:00 Campers gather at the Mess Hall for dinner.

7:30 Divide the kids into two groups. Half will do the craft project; half will play games.

8:00 Groups switch.

8:30 Gather around the campfire—sing songs, make s'mores!

9:00 Good night, campers! Parents pick up the kids. Hand out the goodie bags and favors.

CRAFT NOOK

★ *You can also make bead or button bracelets or decorate painters' hats, which may be easier for younger kids.*

The strategy is to find a project that can be completed in a short time. Have the materials organized and ready and the work space all set to go for the group that arrives first. Backup supplies should be ready for the second group as well.

A typical camp activity is braiding lanyards. If you begin each project (bracelet, key chain, necklace) beforehand, the kids can make real progress and even finish their articles. All unfinished work can be taken home. Lanyard string can be purchased at hobby stores.

LANYARD INSTRUCTIONS

Materials:
two 6-foot pieces of flat vinyl craft lacing; one key ring.

Directions:
Place the two pieces of lacing through the small hole of the key ring with each side being equal. Start the key chain by crossing the strands at the center and doing a square stitch. (This first part requires a bit of coordination and probably some adult help.) Follow the diagrammed instructions, remembering to snug each stitch by pulling strands A and D in one hand and B and C in the other. Keep the tensions uniform in order to make a perfect square. Keep repeating the stitch, following the diagrams, until your key chain is as long as you would like (3 or 4 inches works well). To end the project, tie an overhead knot on each of the four strands. Trim the ends or leave some length and tie a few beads at the end for decoration.

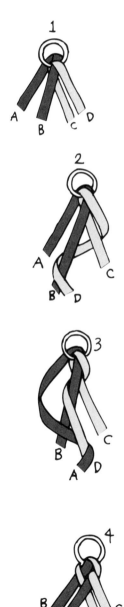

★ *When Andy Israel was 12 years old, his boy scouts troop went on a hiking party with a girl scout troop. What was unusual about this party was that it was an overnight in the winter. Even though it was in California, there was snow on the ground. The party goers decided to build a campfire to keep warm. They did, and it melted the snow underneath, sinking the ground about three feet. What did the ingenious guests do? They leapt into the hole to keep warm.*

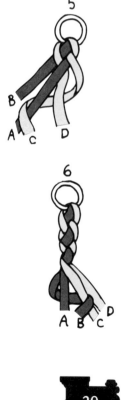

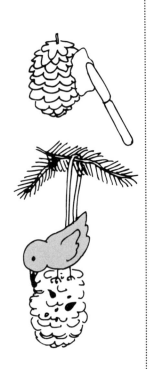

BIRD FEEDER

Gather pine cones for each child. If you're not in a open area where you can find them, they can be purchased at craft stores. Have the children apply peanut butter with plastic knives to their pine cones and then roll them in birdseed. Tie strings to the tops of the cones so the kids can hang them in a tree at home.

The Ackermans made a bird feeder using milk cartons:

Easy-to-make bird feeder:

Use one milk carton for each guest, marking the cutting lines ahead of time. Cut two openings on the carton on opposite sides (follow the lines). Mark an X under each opening and cut. Kids push a dowel through the X hole, through the feeder, and out the other side through the other X hole. Put one of the hemp strings through the hole at the top of the bird feeder and tie a knot in it. That's it!

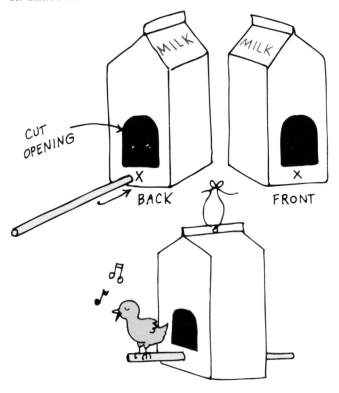

★ *If your children just love sleepovers, have everyone bring sleeping bags. You can rent a large tent, if you like.*

BIRD LEAFLET

On your computer or typewriter, create a bird leaflet to accompany the feeders each guest make and take home. Call a local Audubon or nature society to learn more about the birds that are indigenous to your area. Write a sentence identifying the five or ten most common birds and other wildlife that campers may see in their back yards. On the last page, provide some tips for your bird watchers. For example:

★ Blue jays come around early in the morning or in the late afternoon.

★ Blue jays will scare smaller birds away.

★ Watch for birds from a nearby window. If you get too close, the birds may sense your presence and fly away.

BIRD FEEDING TIPS

★ The best way to attract the birds is with white bread crumbs. Wild birds love the crumbs of baked goods, but you must be careful not to let the crumbs mold, which could cause disease for the little guys.

★ According to the U.S. Fish and Wildlife Service, two of the favorite seeds of wild birds are black-striped sunflower seeds and white prosso millet seeds.

★ Keep a pie tin filled with water on your porch or out in the yard for the birds. They come every day—especially if there is a drought!

★ *When our friend Norman Lear and his son Benjamin, four, decided to camp out in the back yard, they did everything as if they were really in the wild. They pitched a tent, spread out ground cover, cooked dinner over an outdoor fire, and slept under the stars because the sky was so beautiful. But in the middle of the night, very suddenly, it began to pour. Norman and Ben scampered up quickly, clearly disappointed that they wouldn't be able to spend the whole night camping, and ran inside. It took them only a couple of minutes to figure out that the rain was actually the sprinkler system!*

★ *The O'Hallorans have an annual winter "camp-in" reunion with their canoeing friends. The house is set up like an indoor campground, complete with tents, canoe, campfire in the fireplace, and wonderful camp food. They say it does wonders to reduce cabin fever.*

RESOURCES FOR BIRD BOOKS

A Field Guide to the Birds, author Roger Tory Peterson, pub. Houghton Mifflin, 1980
ISBN 0-395-36164-8

The Usborne Book of Bird Facts,
pub. Educational Development Corporation
10302 E. 55th Place, Tulsa, OK 74146
ISBN 0-7460-0619-5

BLOB TAG

No equipment required! The only rule is to stay in the prescribed area, such as the grass in the back yard. Start with one person who is "it." This player must tag someone. When he does, they join hands and have become a Blob. They run together and try to tag another player. Once tagged, the next player holds the hand of the second, and the three become the new Blob and run to tag the next victim. When the Blob attacks its fourth player, the Blob has the power to split into two Blobs. The game continues until all players have been tagged and become part of a Blob. This game, as simple as it sounds, is a lot of fun and can be played over and over again.

GONE FISHING

Equipment needed:
Plastic straws, colored tissue paper fish, and a fish bowl.

Before the party, cut out fish (about 3 inches long) from colored tissue paper—about six to eight fish per guest.

This is a relay game, so divide the guests into two groups. Each participant gets a straw. The first member of each team must inhale through the straw to hold a paper fish in place and transport it from the beginning spot to the fish bowl, 15 to 20 yards away. If a person drops the fish from the straw, he has to start again. The first team to finish wins.

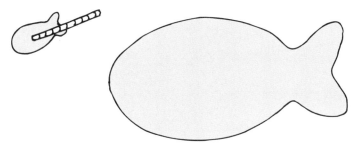

CAMPFIRE SONGS

Use songs from your past camp experience, like "Down by the Old Mill Stream," or collect some favorites from your friends. Change the words whenever you can to make them fit your own Camp Runamok. Rounds are fun and easy to teach—the old favorite "Row, Row, Row Your Boat" is in everyone's repertoire.

Song books for campfire singing:
Tapes in the Wee Sing series come with books filled with all the old favorites. Especially good are the "Wee Sing Sing-Alongs" (formerly titled "Wee Sing Around the Campfire"), "Wee Sing Fun & Folk Songs," and "Wee Sing Silly Songs." Tapes come with sing-along books. If you don't need the tapes, go to the library and check the books out.

FAVORS

Purchase inexpensive flashlights and batteries at any dime store or home center. Using paint pens, write the name of each guest on his or her own flashlight. Camp-themed stickers are also favorites.

And remember to include the crafts made at the party.

★ *Use paper plates, cups, and napkins and plastic utensils for a quick cleanup. Colored or patterned choices make camp more festive.*

MENU

CREAMY COLESLAW
CAMP STEW
S'MORES

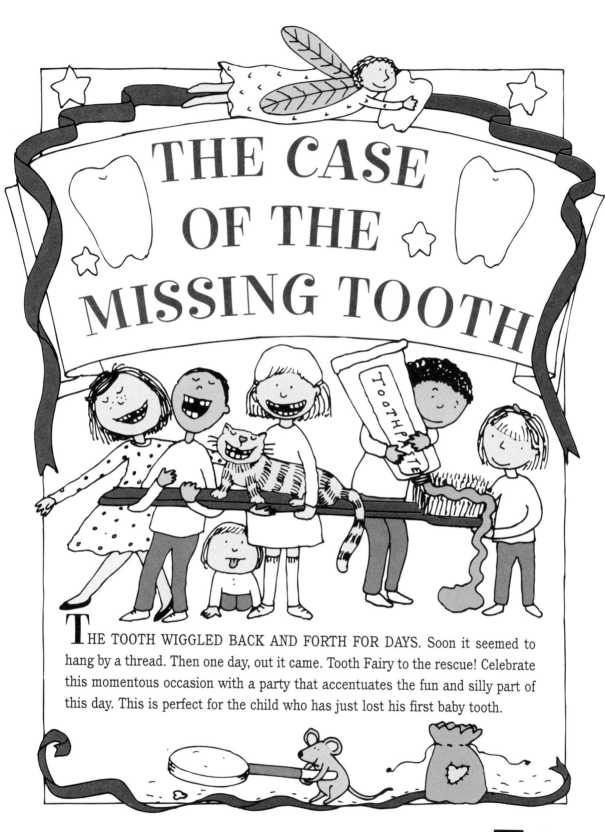

THE CASE OF THE MISSING TOOTH

THE TOOTH WIGGLED BACK AND FORTH FOR DAYS. Soon it seemed to hang by a thread. Then one day, out it came. Tooth Fairy to the rescue! Celebrate this momentous occasion with a party that accentuates the fun and silly part of this day. This is perfect for the child who has just lost his first baby tooth.

INVITATION

Using a white sheet of paper for each invitation, draw an oval shape about 3 inches wide in the center. Cut a slit across the middle (but not touching either side). Now cut out teeth across the bottom and top. When done, cut one of the teeth out completely so it is obvious that one tooth is missing. Now cut out a tongue shape from red paper. Glue to the back of the mouth with the tongue sticking out through the teeth.

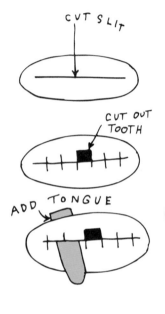

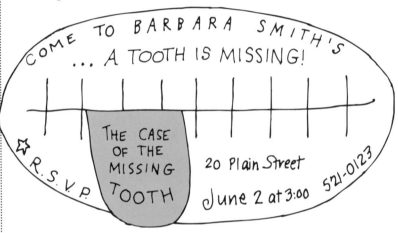

DECORATIONS

Draw a large tooth; cut out and make several to hang around the room. Collect portraits out of magazines and black out a tooth on each. Hang them around the room.

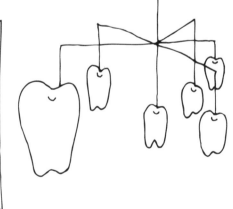

ACTIVITIES

TREASURED TEETH HUNT

Hide jelly beans and one travel-size toothpaste. Whoever finds the most beans gets a prize, as does the player who finds the tube of toothpaste and the guest who finds the most jelly beans of one color.

BLACKOUT

All the guests put blackout on one of their teeth so they can all pretend they've lost a tooth. Take instant-developing pictures of each guest and have them color in the teeth in different colors with markers. Display the photos around the room until the guests are ready to take them home.

TOOTH POUCH

★ *Take turns making pouches and rolling ice cream, because rolling the ice cream for more than ten minutes is too difficult for young kids.*

Make a velvet tooth pouch for a party favor. Cut velvet squares 3 inches square. Using a sewing machine, sew three sides of two squares together, wrong sides out. Turn top down and finish the edge. Turn right side out. Cut ¼-inch slits ½ inch down from the top edge. Make one tooth pouch for each guest. Purchase ribbons in different colors and let the guests thread their choice of ribbons between the slits.

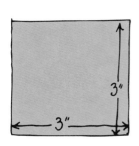
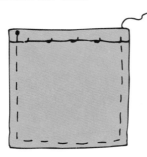
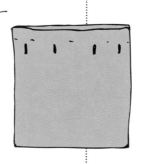

★ *Buy extra ice cream to serve, because the ice cream the kids make won't be enough for everyone.*

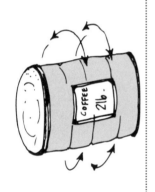

MAKING ICE CREAM

Kids love to make their own ice cream. Here is an ice cream that is made as you watch—kids think it is really miraculous. You will need:

> 1 cup milk
> 1 cup heavy cream
> ½ cup sugar
> ½ teaspoon vanilla extract
> Crushed ice (large pieces)
> Rock salt

Put the milk, heavy cream, sugar, and vanilla in a 1-pound coffee can. Close the lid tightly. Put the entire can into a 5-pound coffee can. Pack the section around the smaller can with crushed ice and rock salt (you may want to wear rubber gloves because your hands get cold from handling the ice). Close the can tightly.

Now have guests take turns rolling the can back and forth on a hard floor, between two pairs of children about 4 feet apart, for 10 minutes (and again for another 10 minutes). Have each set of children roll it back and forth for about 4 minutes (you can get another timer) so they won't get bored and all the children will get a chance to roll the can. To double the yield, you can have two cans going at the same time and keep eight children busy. After ten minutes, open the outer can and throw out the rock salt and what will be melted ice. Open the inner can and mix everything together (be sure to scrape sides of the can). Replace the lid and again pack with ice and more rock salt. Roll again for 10 minutes. When done, the ice cream will be quite soft. Let the children have a taste, then put it in the freezer until you are ready to serve.

HOT TOOTH

If the Tooth Fairy hasn't already taken your child's baby tooth away, use the missing tooth in this tooth tag game (you can also use a penny).

Have the kids sit on the floor in a circle. Play a tape of your child's favorite music. The object is to pass the tooth around from hand to hand. When the music stops, whoever is left holding the tooth is out. The winner is the child left who has managed to avoid holding the tooth whenever the music stops.

FAVORS

Unusual toothbrushes

Bubble-gum-flavored toothpaste

Tooth pouch

Chattering teeth wind-ups

MENU

CHEESE TORTILLAS
BLUE CORN CHIPS
BABY TOOTH COOKIES
HOMEMADE ICE CREAM

★ *July 6 is the Festival of the Tooth in Sri Lanka (formerly Ceylon). Once a year, the 2½-inch eyetooth of Buddha is paraded in the city of Kandy. It is enclosed in jewels and silver. The festival continues for ten days, with parades of jeweled elephants and many dancers every night. Spectators come from all over the country.*
At the end of the festival, the tooth is returned to the Temple of the Tooth and enclosed again in its silver shrine.

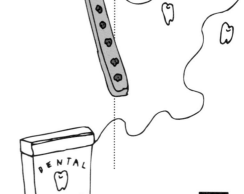

39

DAY OF THE DRAGON

CELEBRATIONS OF THE CHINESE NEW YEAR are full of fascinating traditions, revelry, and beautiful costumes, which intrigue children. When Brenda Sure was twelve, her mom, Sally, helped her create a Chinese New Year's party where everyone was asked to come dressed as a dragon. This dragon festival included a parade around the neighborhood in the tradition of the holiday, because Brenda thought that all her friends' creativity should have a chance to be seen. Although the actual Chinese New Year occurs at a specific time each year, your celebration can take place whenever you feel dragonish!

INVITATION

You'll need wooden or bamboo chopsticks, which can be bought at well-stocked grocery and cooking supply stores or at a local Chinese restaurant. Write the party information on the outside wrapper. Decide whether you want the guests to come in costume, and include such instructions in the invitation (for example, "Come Dressed as a Dragon").

★ *Gung Bay Fat Chow is the Chinese way to say "Happy New Year." But when translated literally, it means "Wish You Make a Lot of Money."*

DRAGON PARTY ◇ February 10th AT 6:00 pm
50 Pine Street
at DALEY ACKERMAN'S R.S.V.P. 555 - 1212

DECORATIONS

Stores in local Oriental neighborhoods are full of exquisite decorations you can use to create your environment. You will find an assortment of lanterns that will look great hung around the party room. They are very inexpensive, so buy them in quantity (one or two lanterns will get lost in a room—you will need many to create a great effect). Paper fans, which come in many colors and designs, can be hung and also spread around the dinner table. Masks make gorgeous decorations, and Oriental kites can be hung inside and outside the party area. All of these decorations—lanterns, fans, masks, kites—can be used as favors or prizes as well.

A resource for chopsticks, lanterns, and lots of other party favors is the Oriental Trading Company in Omaha, Nebraska: (800) 228-2269. Just call for a free catalog.

★ *The highlight of a Chinese New Year parade is the Parade of the Golden Dragon, held on the first night of the new year. Everyone is dressed in extravagant satin costumes. The centerpiece of the parade is a block-long golden dragon, made of silks, satin, and velvet in bright colors. Under it are twenty or so men who make the dragon weave to and fro in the street. The dragon is a symbol of strength.*

ACTIVITIES

CHARADES

This game is adapted from the old Chinese custom of telling fortunes with bamboo sticks. Use an old cigar box or a container of about the same size. Paint it red. Fill it with colored cellophane straws into each of which you have placed a tightly rolled New Year's resolution written on thin tracing paper. Be sure there are at least as many straws as guests (make a couple of extras, just in case). Divide the guests into two teams. When each of your guests has drawn a straw, the first person who drew acts out his resolution in front of his teammates. The team must guess the resolution within three minutes to score a point. Keep going until everyone has had a turn to act out his resolution. The team with the most points wins. An appropriate prize might be Chinese fortune-telling fish (available at novelty stores or at Penny Whistle stores).

Here are some suggestions:

★ I will do my homework before dinner every night.

★ I will fold all the laundry without being told to.

★ I will keep my elbows off the dinner table.

★ I will keep my room neat.

★ I will walk and feed the dog all by myself.

★ I will bundle up the newspapers for recycling.

★ I will take out the recycling for my parents.

★ I will wash my parents' car.

★ I will mow the lawn for free.

PITCHING CARDS

This is a version of an old Chinese gambling game in which players tossed coins into holes in the ground. For this updated version, you need two decks of cards and two hats or boxes. Give the players five minutes to practice, and then start the game. Have each guest take turns tossing cards into the hats or boxes. Each player has five chances at a time. Players score one point each time they get a card into the hat. Keep a total of each player's score, and award a prize to the player with the highest score.

★ *You can also keep score by adding up the face value of the cards.*

DRAGON STREAMERS

Making a dragon streamer, or *Chin Jie*, is a great activity to include as part of your celebration. On a sheet of poster board or cardboard, draw a dragon's head. Using paints or markers, color the dragon and cut it out. Next, cut a strip of cardboard and staple it to the underside of the head for a holder. Staple streamers or ribbons to the back of the head. When you run holding the head, the streamers will float and flow like the body of an angry dragon.

★ *Jacks, a favorite American pastime, is an old Chinese game that makes a good time filler or party favor.*

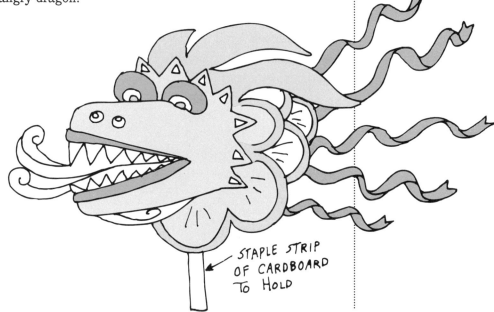

STAPLE STRIP OF CARDBOARD TO HOLD

★ *To help you determine*
what additional animal to add
to your dragon theme, here
are the animals that are
venerated in these years:

The year of the rat:
1996, 2008

The year of the ox:
1997, 2009

The year of the tiger:
1998, 2010

The year of the hare:
1999, 2011

The year of the dragon:
2000, 2012

The year of the snake:
2001, 2013

The year of the horse:
2002, 2014

The year of the ram:
2003, 2015

The year of the monkey:
2004, 2016

The year of the cockerel:
2005, 2017

The year of the dog:
2006, 2018

The year of the pig:
2007, 2019

CONFUSION

Divide the guests into pairs. Two children sit on the floor back to back and lock their arms. The first to get to his feet without unlinking arms is the winner. The winners of the first round then match up with each other, and play continues until the final round with the last two players. Give a prize to the ultimate winner.

CATCHING THE DRAGON'S TAIL

This game is similar to Crack the Whip. The guests place their hands on each other's shoulders, forming a line. The first child is the dragon's head; the last one its tail. With the line intact, the dragon's head attempts to catch its tail. When the first child succeeds, he goes to the end of the line as the tail, and so on.

TONGUE TIED

This is a game in which new words are formed by starting with the last syllable of the preceding word named. For instance, a player says "dreadful." The person to his left says "fulfill," the next says "filter," then "termite," and so on, until a player gets stuck and is out of the game. Continue playing until there is a winner.

PARADE WITH DRAGON CENTIPEDE

Making a dragon with all the kids is a lot of fun. Sew two old white sheets together with a hole in front for the leader's head. Let the children decorate it with markers, glue, sequins, ribbons, and crepe paper. To make a more sophisticated dragon, make a papier-mâché dragon head using chicken wire as a base. (This, of course, must be done well in advance of the party!) One guest wears the dragon head as a hat, with his own head sticking out from the hole. Other guests crouch under the sheet with their legs sticking out. If you are going to have a parade, this is one dragon that will make an impact in the neighborhood!

★ *If you have a copier available, make copies of the Chinese year chart so each guest can take his "year" home.*

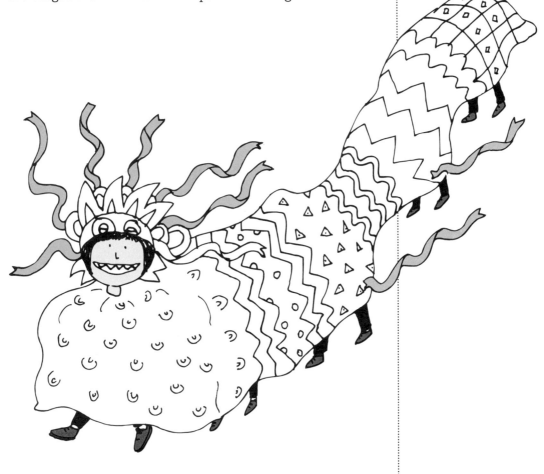

45

CHOPSTICKS TWEEZERS

When Marc was little, he really wanted to eat with chopsticks, but his little hands couldn't handle them. One evening when the Gilbars were at a Chinese restaurant, a young waitress made chopstick tweezers for Marc, explaining that very young Chinese children often use them. Marc was astounded and thrilled that he could eat with chopsticks, and he made sure everyone in the restaurant could see him performing this great feat.

★ *Dominoes, Chinese checkers, Rummy O, Jacks: Set any or all of these games up on tables around the room for guests to play when they first arrive or at any time throughout the party.*

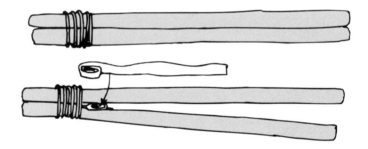

Make these chopstick tweezers as you sit down to your New Year's festival, and use them to eat dinner. Before the food is brought to the table, everyone will be making eating utensils. Give each child a pair of wooden chopsticks and a rubber band. Don't throw away the paper wrappers—they're essential to the end product. Wrap the end you hold with a rubber band as tightly as you can. Take the paper and fold it until it is about ½ inch long. Stick it between the chopsticks at the end with the rubber band. The result is tweezers that look like chopsticks and make even the most uncoordinated look impressive. They are especially popular with very young kids who cannot imagine that they, too, could eat with chopsticks!

MENU

Here are some favorite dishes to prepare if you have time and/or the inclination. But don't hesitate to order takeout if you have a good local Chinese restaurant that delivers. It's often more economical! Remember to have your guests use chopsticks to eat with—now that they have their newly made "tweezers," this becomes easy for everyone.

FORTUNE COOKIES

JENNY'S PEANUT BUTTER NOODLES

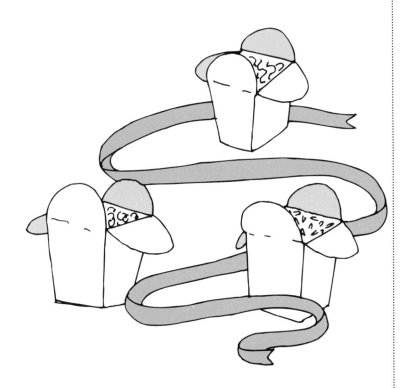

EARTH DAY

IT MAY BE THE BIRD'S NEST APPEARING outside your kitchen window that grabs your attention. Maybe it's just a change in the weather. There simply are days, especially in the spring, that call out for recognition. Be prepared to acknowledge the return of spring with an Earth Day celebration.

INVITATION

Buy seed packets for flowers and vegetables that can be grown in your area. Write the party information with Magic Marker on the package. Mail in a padded envelope.

COVER THE SEED COPY WITH A WHITE LABEL

ACTIVITIES

MAKING A TERRARIUM

What you need:
One glass or plastic jar for each guest, small stones, sand, dirt, small plants (like ferns and ivy). Cover the bottom of the jar with the stones, a layer of sand, and then a thick layer of dirt. Poke in small plants. Include instructions to water plants only when necessary. To create a "rain forest" environment, tops can be covered with plastic wrap and removed when too much moisture accumulates, otherwise terrarium tops can be left off.

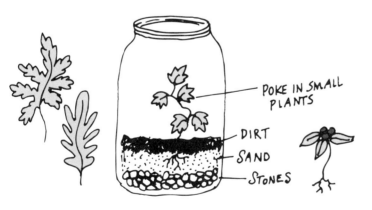

POKE IN SMALL PLANTS

DIRT

SAND

STONES

★ *Pinching plants back will make them full and beautiful.*

★ *Plant herbs or mini-vegetables that thrive indoors—scallions, parsley, sage, basil.*

come to Jessica's

APRIL 22nd at NOON
12 JONES RD
555-1234

RSVP

COVER BACK OF SEED PACKET WITH WHITE LABEL

WRITE PARTY COPY ON BACK OF SEED PACKET

★ *Sand saucers spruce up any table. Use old clay saucers or foil plates and fill them with sand, flowers, leaves, seeds, shells, feathers—any natural objects. Keep them moist to keep the flowers and leaves fresh.*

★ *A local nursery dumped a truckload of topsoil meant for spring planting on Diane Koge-Anders's front lawn in Castle Rock, Colorado, instead of in the back yard where it belonged. She conned the neighborhood kids into bringing over their play wheelbarrows to move it to the back. (She kept telling them that she could hear Mother Earth thanking them for making her stomach feel better!)*

★ *Organize a party around planting time in your garden. The planting of rosebushes, shrubs, and trees offers an excellent occasion for a gathering of friends to participate and celebrate.*

MAKE YOUR OWN COMPASS

You need a darning needle, a magnet, a cork, and a dish or bowl of water for each compass. Rub the ends of the magnet across the needle about fifty times, always going in the same direction. This magnetizes the needle. Push the needle into the cork and lay it in the dish of water. Try moving the cork in several different directions. Experiment to see which way the needle points and under what conditions.

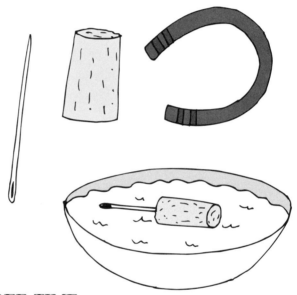

TREE TIME

Here's an easy pad-and-pencil game: What kinds of things come from trees? Ask your guests to try to name as many items as they can in one minute. The guest with the most responses is the winner. A good party favor is a tree product such as a novelty wooden pencil or chewing gum.

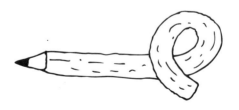

WHEELBARROW RACE

Divide the guests into teams of two. Set up start and finish lines. At the sound of "Go," one person in each pair grabs the feet of the other, who propels himself by using his arms to walk. At the finish line, players switch places and return to the starting line. The pair that makes it back first is the winner.

TREE SHIRTS

Using the Penny Whistle pictures you see here, make your own stencils for T-shirts with a natural style. Give every guest a blank T-shirt and have fabric paints, sponges, and pieces of cardboard on hand. Insert a piece of cardboard in the T-shirt, position the stencil on the T-shirt, and, using the sponges, dab paint evenly onto the shirt and around the edges of the stencil. You may want to tape the stencil on the shirt in order to hold it in place. Let the shirts dry completely, and advise guests to iron the shirts when they get home to set the paint before they wash them.

★ *The real Earth Day is celebrated on April 22. Arbor Day may vary but is usually observed on the last Friday in April.*

★ *You can buy a kit to make your own chewing gum at most toy stores (or order from Penny Whistle).*

PLACE STENCIL OVER T-SHIRT, PAINT ON THE SHIRT INSIDE STENCIL.

CUT OUT STENCIL

INSERT CARDBOARD INSIDE THE T-SHIRT

FINISHED SHIRT

★ *Gather one or more children for a special outing to watch the sunrise. Locate a good hilltop ahead of time so you can have an unrestricted view, and find out what time the sunrise will be.*

CLEAN-UP PICTURE

Photocopy our "what's-wrong-with-this-picture" drawing and hand out the copies. Set a time limit and have the children circle everything that doesn't belong. The child who finds the most litter wins. There are more than 15 things that are not ecologically correct to find in the drawing.

LEAF RUBBINGS

Place a bunch of leaves under a piece of paper. Have the children rub the paper with the side of a crayon. The result will be an abstract drawing of the leaves.

FAVORS

365 Ways to Clean Up the Planet or a similar book

T-shirts that the kids have made

Bug viewers bought at a nature store

MENU

Brown-bag the lunches for a picnic, indoors or out. If you plan to cook outside, substitute the Barbecued Chicken Cheeseburgers for the Maple Leaf Sandwiches.

MAPLE LEAF SANDWICHES OR BARBECUED
CHICKEN CHEESEBURGERS

SWEET POTATO CHIPS

MINI CARROTS

CHOCOLATE CAKE

BUG JUICE

CARDBOARD DRINK BOXES FOR THE PICNIC
(OR A BUG PUNCH)

★ *Many Seattle school-children raise salmon in fish tanks for later release into a stream. Often a class will use the release date as an occasion to celebrate with local Native American tribes with storytellers, drummers, and singers as the fish swim away.*

EGGSTRAVAGANZA

WHEN YOU LOVE TO DECORATE EGGS, and relish finding new ways to create unforgettable designs, it's hard to wait for that once-a-year holiday. So forget the rule and plan an egg-decorating festival at any time of year. Or be a traditionalist and have an eggstravaganza right before Easter. There are many different ways to decorate eggs, some of which result in eggs you can keep as mementos forever.

INVITATION

Copy our basket below. Make a paper spring by cutting out a spiral from paper. Cut an egg out of paper and color it with markers. Glue the egg to the end of the paper spring and attach the other end of the spring to the basket. Now color in the basket with pastel markers, and you have an invitation.

You can write the copy on the basket itself or on the other eggs you drew in the basket.

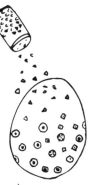

★ *You can also put glitter on the egg, or if you make the egg out of heavier paper (like cardboard or foam board), you can even glue tiny plastic beads to cover the egg.*

ATTACH A REAL RIBBON

CUT OUT

Come to the RILEYS' at 2:00

April 10
2 Depot Lane
123-4567
♡ R.S.V.P.

EGGSTRAVAGANZA PARTY

CUT A SPIRAL

GLUE TO BASKET

GLUE SPIRAL TO BACK OF EGG

DECORATIONS

EGG TREE

Making an egg tree is a Pennsylvania Dutch custom. The tree is fun and easy to make and may be used as a centerpiece for your party. Remove the leaves from a sturdy tree branch and set in a base, which can be a box or can filled with florist's clay or green foam. If you like, you can spray-paint the branch before you place it in the base. Attach blown-out and decorated eggs to the branches. A loop of ribbon or string glued with a glue gun to the broad side of the egg will serve as a hanger (or you can work one end of a pipe cleaner about 1 inch into the top hole in the egg, bend the pipe cleaner to form a hanger, and then hang your eggs on the tree).

★ *Make your dyed eggs shine by putting a few drops of vegetable oil on a cloth and rubbing the eggs.*

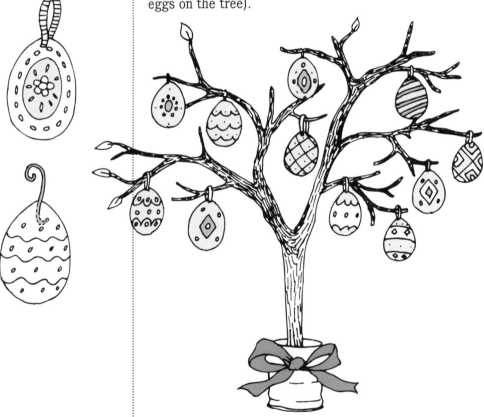

DECORATING EGGS

HOW TO BLOW OUT AN EGG

Before you decorate your eggs, you can blow them out so you can keep them. Carefully prick both ends with an egg pick or a heated pin or needle. Hold the egg over a bowl and blow from one end just as you would blow up a balloon until all the liquid is emptied.

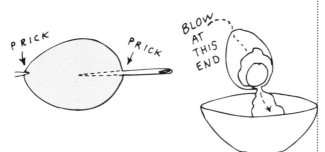

★ When our friend Mary Murphy and her daughter Megen Swertlow tried some of these unique decorating techniques, the results so enchanted them that they not only saved their creations but began to collect decorated eggs of all kinds. At last sight, Mary and Megen were seen scouting the local swap meets for any eggs they could find!

USING NATURAL DYES

Natural dyes produce different shades of colors than the commercial dyes you can buy in stores.

For yellow, try saffron, daffodils, yellow onion skins, or crocuses.

For green, use broccoli, spinach, moss, rhubarb, or grass.

For blue, use blueberries.

For brown, use coffee, tea, walnut shells, or plums.

For red, use beets or red cabbage.

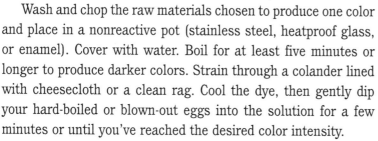

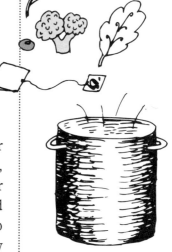

Wash and chop the raw materials chosen to produce one color and place in a nonreactive pot (stainless steel, heatproof glass, or enamel). Cover with water. Boil for at least five minutes or longer to produce darker colors. Strain through a colander lined with cheesecloth or a clean rag. Cool the dye, then gently dip your hard-boiled or blown-out eggs into the solution for a few minutes or until you've reached the desired color intensity.

★ *Younger children can decorate eggs without the hazard of shells breaking by using plastic eggs.*

EASY DECORATING FOR YOUNGER CHILDREN

It can be difficult and frustrating for younger children to decorate eggs with painting and sophisticated designs that are quite doable for older kids and adults. Here are some ways these youngsters can enjoy creating their own jewels:

Glue used postage stamps to your dyed eggs.

Hold the egg carefully in whichever hand you don't use for writing. With the other hand, using markers, create random patterns of dots, dashes, swirls, or lines over the eggs. Let each color dry completely before using the next.

Paste on different seals or stickers of favorite sports teams or other logos.

Stick vinyl letters to the egg.

Write your name on the egg.

Use binder reinforcement rings: stick them to the egg, then dip the egg in commercial dye. When the egg is dry, remove the seals and you'll have a colored egg with little white circles all over it.

CHOCOLATE NEST

Here's an easy way to make a chocolate box to hold jelly beans (also called "mini-eggs" by very young 'uns). Melt 1 teaspoon Crisco with one bag of chocolate chips (it will look like a spreadable frosting). Pour into the smallest brown paper bag (with a flat bottom) and form a chocolate box by pressing the chocolate to the sides with a spatula to form the box inside the bottom of the paper bag, making sure the chocolate goes up the sides of the bag an inch or two so your box has sides to it. Refrigerate for about an hour. After the chocolate has hardened, remove the bag and fill it with jelly beans. This recipe, using one bag of chocolate chips, will make either one or two chocolate baskets, depending on the size of the paper bag and the depth of the basket.

★ *The Chocolate Nest is the creation of Susan Russell. She says that if you crinkle the bag, you'll get crinkled chocolate.*

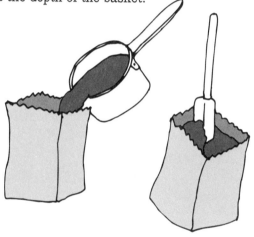

MAKE A CLAY NEST

Using self-hardening clay, form a nest with your hands and let it harden. Kids can use this as an alternative to a basket.

★ *For an Easter egg coloring party, have assorted materials on hand like construction paper, glue, felt, yarn, ribbon, lace, pipe cleaners, glitter, foil, colored pens, and the like so that everyone's imagination can run wild.*

MARBLEIZED EGGS

Blow out the egg as described above. Mix a drop of white paint with your chosen color of washable acrylic paint and paint each egg using a sponge brush. With a piece of sponge, dab full-strength paint to create a marbled effect. You can form veins with a feather. Let dry. When done, you can still add designs with markers, or leave the eggs plain.

RIBBON EGGS

Run a glue stick over the dull side of four strips of ¼-inch satin ribbon. Starting at the top, wrap the ribbons around a hard-boiled egg. You can even glue on a bow! To make a Marc's "crazy egg," just glue on one 2-foot strip of ribbon in a random pattern.

CARTOON EGGS

Cut out your favorite cartoon characters and glue to the egg. Spray with shellac.

STICKER MAGIC

Use stickers in different shapes and sizes. Stick them to a blown-out egg that has been dipped into any dye.

OTHER ACTIVITIES

MAKING A BUNNY EGG

You can make the dough in this project ahead of time so it will be ready for the children, or you can all make it together at the party.

Dye your egg. Remove the crust from a slice of white bread and crumble the bread into a cup. Add a tablespoon of white glue and knead until it is a smooth paste—this is your dough. If the dough is too sticky, add a little flour; if it is too dry, add a few drops of liquid soap. Now add pink poster paint to the dough and mix well. (If you are making this ahead of time, put the dough in a plastic bag until you are ready to use it.)

Use the dough to form the head, ears, and tail. Draw a face on the bunny's head. Using the glue gun, attach the head, ears, and tail to the egg.

GLUE

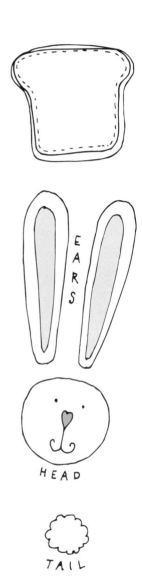

EARS

HEAD

TAIL

★ *Greek festive tradition includes a special Easter-egg-cracking game called egg knocking, based on a belief that an egg is the symbol of life and you must crack it open to release the blessings. Two people take turns playing this game with hard-boiled eggs. Players hold the eggs with the pointed end facing out and knock them against each other until one breaks. The holder of the unbroken egg will have good luck throughout the year.*

NUMBER EGG HUNT

Collect colored eggs (at least triple the number of guest players) and write numbers on each with a marker. Hide the eggs. The guests hunt for the eggs. At the end of the hunt, each guest adds up the numbers on his eggs. The one with the highest total wins.

A variation on this is to use different colored eggs with no numbers on them. But have a chart ready where each color has a numbered value (e.g., red is four points, green is ten points—you can even hide one gold egg worth 100 points). At the end of this hunt, each guest has to figure out his total by comparing the colors he has collected with their worth on the chart and adding them up.

EGG ROLL

This is our favorite game ever, and one reason why we began giving Eggstravaganza parties at other times of the year. It's just too much fun to wait for Easter to have this egg roll!

For this game you need blown eggs, one for each player. Reinforce the blown eggshells by covering the holes with notebook paper hole reinforcements. This will make the shells strong enough to be used quite a few times. Lay out a course, either indoors or outdoors, having a plainly marked starting line and a finish line 30 or 40 feet away. Place an eggshell for each player on the starting line. To give enough room for movement, the shells should be 3 feet apart. When ready, each player kneels behind his eggshell. When you yell "GO," each player tries to blow his eggshell across the finish line. He must obey these rules:

★ The player must stay on his hands and knees.

★ The egg must be moved only by blowing.

★ The egg must not be blown so hard that it rolls end over end.

Any player who breaks one of these rules (or the eggshell) is given a penalty of 5 feet back.

A variation on this game is to roll or push the eggs toward a shallow hole. A large tin can or milk carton turned on its side can also be used as a target.

Another variation is to have players roll the egg from the starting line to the finish line using only their nose.

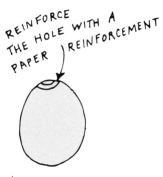

REINFORCE THE HOLE WITH A PAPER REINFORCEMENT

★ *Egg rolling was originally a reminder of the stone that was rolled away from Christ's tomb.*

EGG RUNNING

For this relay race you need a teaspoon for each player and two raw eggs per team. Set up starting and finish lines. Divide the players into two teams. Give each player a teaspoon. Each player should hold the spoon by the handle—between his teeth! The players in each team line up behind the lead egg runner. Place an egg in the bowl of the spoon held by the lead egg runner in each team. At the sound of "GO" the lead runners move toward the finish line and back to the starting line, and keeping their hands clasped behind their backs and without dropping the eggs, transfer their eggs to the next players' spoons without using their hands. Each team member takes his turn until every player has successfully run the race. The team finishing first is declared the winner. A player who drops the egg from his spoon without cracking it may pick it up, go back to the starting line, and begin again. If it's cracked, the player is out!

BALLOON EGG RELAYS

Divide children into two teams and line them up. Each team gets a balloon egg. The first player in each line tosses the "egg" in the air and bats it with the palm of his hand, batting it toward a far wall. The "egg" must not be carried. When the "egg" hits the wall, the player can seize it and run back to the next player in line, who bats the "egg" to the wall. The first line to finish wins.

For younger children, use balloons as "eggs" for a relay adventure.

GERMAN EGG GAME

Two baskets, paper, grass, and hard-boiled eggs are needed to play the German Egg Game. Two teams are lined up, one called the Bunny team and the other the Rabbit team. One team tends the baskets; the other team tends to the running. While player 1 of the Bunny team runs to a goal and back, player 1 of the Rabbit team takes the eggs from one basket, one at a time, using only one hand, and places them in the other basket. If the runner gets back before the eggs are all transferred, he scores a point for his team; if not, the team with the baskets wins a point. The next two in line now compete.

Note: In planning the location of the goal, the distance between the baskets, and the number of eggs to be used, experiment before playing at the party so as to create an environment that will be fun and competitive but not frustrating for guests. Keep score as play continues. When all players have had a turn, have the teams change responsibilities and keep score until the end. Total each team's points. The team with the highest score wins.

★ *For an extra-special Easter basket, add small favors like stickers, bunny-shaped erasers, and rubber stamps.*

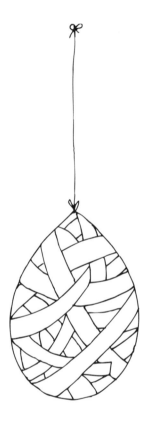

EGG PIÑATA

Buy a balloon that will blow up to about 18 inches in diameter. After blowing up the balloon, tie a knot in its neck and attach a long piece of string to it. Hang the balloon from a fixture or hanger. Cover the balloon with four or five layers of papier-mâché. After the papier-mâché has completely dried, puncture the balloon with a pin and remove it from the inside of the piñata. Enlarge the hole at the top and fill the piñata with small gifts. Tie a network of heavy twine around the piñata with the long ends gathered at the top. Now apply more papier-mâché over the twine. When this second coating is thoroughly dry, decorate the piñata with paint and crepe-paper streamers.

Now that the piñata is made, tie a length of clothesline to the strings at the top so the piñata can be suspended from the ceiling. To play, blindfold the first player and give him a stick so he can try to strike the piñata. Have several players take turns until someone has shattered the papier-mâché and spilled the gifts for everyone to share.

JELLY BEAN GAME

Give each player two toothpicks and two shallow paper cups. One cup is full of jelly beans. At a signal, players begin transferring jelly beans from the full cup to the empty cup, using only their toothpicks. The hard part is that you may not stab or pierce the jellybeans while moving them from cup to cup. The winner is the player who transfers the most candy without stab marks within a given amount of time. For a variation, younger kids might play this game without a time limit. Older kids might do elimination rounds where the playing period becomes shorter and shorter until the ultimate winner is announced.

MENU

EGG NESTS

BASKET OF MINIATURE VEGETABLES

BUNNY BREAD

COOKIE BONNETS

EASTER BUNNY BREAD

★ *When the Root kids were little and having annual Easter egg hunts, their parents would use little plastic eggs and put coins in them. As the kids got older and got bored with what they considered to be a kid's Easter egg hunt, dad Irv kept upping the stakes to keep up the kids' interest in the hunts. The kids are now in their thirties, and this past year, Irv put five- and ten-dollar bills (even one twenty) in the plastic Easter eggs. The "kids" kept their interest in Easter egg hunts!*

FRIDAY THE 13TH

ANYTIME A FRIDAY AND THE 13TH DAY of the month coincide, you have the perfect excuse for a party. Superstition influences many people, indicating bad luck on this date. Your party turns this notion into a "This could be your lucky day" theme.

INVITATION

Send a horseshoe or four-leaf clover drawings. Attach a note that reads: "This could be your lucky day! Join (name) for a Friday the 13th party."

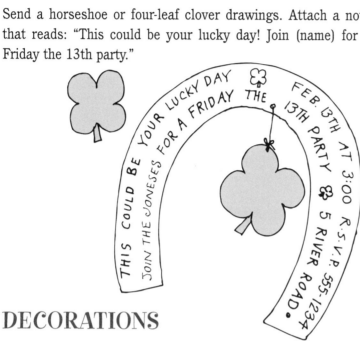

DECORATIONS

Use lucky symbols like four-leaf clovers around the party room. For an atmosphere meant to "spook" everyone, borrow ideas from Halloween (see *The Penny Whistle Halloween Book*). Dim the lights, or substitute blue light bulbs for your regular ones. Play ghoulish music in the background. Place ladders around the house. Put black cats on tables.

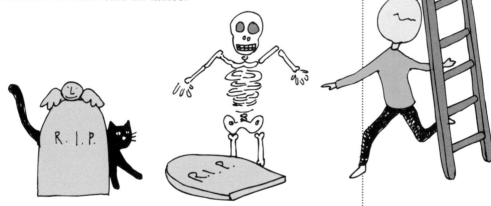

★ *Use real plaster of paris. Homemade plasters made with flour, salt, and water are much too gooey and don't dry properly for this project. Buy the real thing!*

★ *In using plaster of paris, you don't need large objects or jeans. Children's or doll clothes will work just as well.*

Our favorite decoration is a pair of plaster-of-paris jeans that stand on their own. Buy plaster of paris at any medical supply store. The 5-pound package comes with instructions. Use several pairs of old overalls or jeans—all pieces of clothing that you are prepared to never use again. Dip each into plaster of paris. Hang them to dry. Stuff with newspaper and brush over with another coat of plaster of paris. The result will be free-standing sculptures that look as haunting as any ghost you've ever seen! Group them together or stand them in different parts of the room.

ACTIVITIES

MAKE A SNAKE

This project takes a day or more to dry, so if you make several snakes ahead of time, your guests can decorate them after they've finished the papier-mâché part.

What you need:
Newspaper, blank newsprint (or the paper from an inexpensive drawing pad), a wire clothes hanger, 1½-inch-wide masking tape, flour, salt, and water. Tear the newspaper into strips about 1 inch wide.

Making Paste
    ½ cup flour
    1 tablespoon salt
    1 cup warm water

Mix ingredients in a large bowl with your hands until consistency is that of a creamed soup. Add more flour or water to thicken or thin paste as needed.

★ *You can also make a snake out of stockings—just use a glue gun to glue on buttons for eyes.*

★ *Line the paste bowl with plastic wrap. When you have finished the project, throw the lining away for a quick clean-up.*

KEEP SOME CURVES

BEND THE COAT HANGER TO MAKE THE FRAME OF THE SNAKE

71

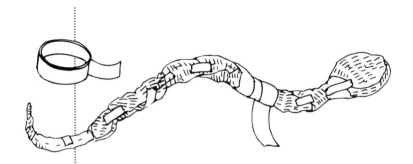

Bend the coat hanger until it is straightened out except for the hook. You may want to keep some curves or waves to be part of the snake's body. Tape crumpled newspaper to the hanger until the body is formed. Use less paper to make a pointed tail. Use a ball of paper to form the head, or two balls of paper to form a head with an open mouth taped to the hook. Next, dip a strip of newspaper into paste and remove the excess with your fingers. Wrap the strip around the snake. Continue to wrap the strips, overlapping each piece until the snake has been covered two times. Add a third layer of blank newsprint strips. Allow papier-mâché snake to dry—remember, it may take more than one day. Paint or decorate it. Cut eyes and a forked tongue from cardboard, paint them, and glue them to your snake. Acrylic paints are the best to use.

HORSESHOES

This good old-fashioned game can be set up in the back yard or played indoors if it is the rubber kind.

SUPERSTITION

This is a pen-and-pencil game. How many superstitions can the guests recall in one minute? Some examples:

★ *Make socks into plaster-of-paris centerpieces! Make sure the bottom of the sock is flat when drying, insert a plastic bag with water, and add flowers!*

★ Don't walk under a ladder.

★ Don't cross the path of a black cat.

★ Don't open an umbrella indoors.

★ Don't leave a hat on the table.

GIVE 'EM A HAND

For this project you'll need an inexpensive pair of *plain* cotton gloves for each guest and a variety of decorations such as fake fingernails, glue, sequins, fake fur, fabric, puff paint, markers, and buttons.

Let your guests create a pair of ghoulish hands. Draw wrinkles with a pen on the fingers. Glue on hair to make a scary hand, or make a glittery one with the addition of sequins, fake nails, and lace.

73

MONSTER MANIA

For this activity, you'll need one Pez dispenser per person and Das clay (that's the kind that hardens in the air) in a variety of colors. Allow your guest to create their own monster Pez by having them mold a new head on the existing dispenser top (just make sure they don't cover the spring mechanism that allows the mouth to open and close, thus spitting out candy).

★ *Wheat paste (wallpaper paste) is excellent for making papier-mâché.*

FAVORS

Ghoulish hands

Pez dispensers

Dice

MENU

NIGHT CRAWLERS

ABRACADABRA

LUCKY ROLL-UPS

GHOULISH GUACAMOLE

SKELETON COOKIES

GO FLY A KITE

IT FEELS IRRESISTIBLE! The wind is blowing and the air is soft. The hobbyists are out in the park making it look so easy to get that bright piece of cloth triangle aloft. Your kids are eager to try it, too, so you decide to go for it.

Kite flying is an art and a skill. Whether you are very young or a bit older, flying a kite takes patience and can be a challenge for the most talented among us. This party includes making a simple kite that anyone should be able to fly on a windy day. But in case the wind is low, or if the flying is shaky, we have also included several kites that are more decorative than flyable and will make any child's wall an eye-catching treat!

INVITATION

This is a great spur-of-the-moment event, but if you are planning ahead, make the invitation on a Frisbee. Glue an 8- to 10-inch ribbon to one end for a tail. Mail or deliver.

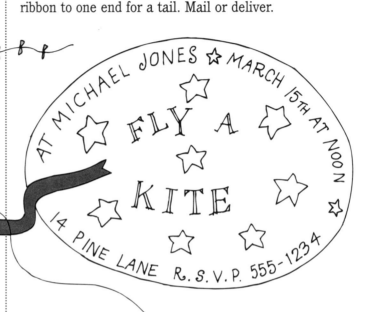

AT MICHAEL JONES ☆ MARCH 15TH AT NOON
FLY A KITE
14 PINE LANE R.S.V.P. 555-1234

ACTIVITIES

Kite flying takes some skill, so invite adults and/or older kids with some kite flying experience to participate. Here are instructions for creating homemade kites. And if you don't want to fly them, just hang them on the wall!

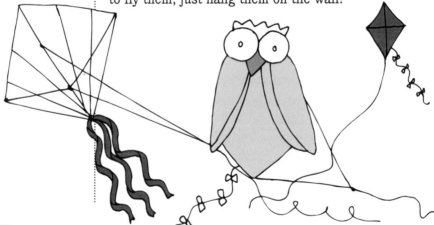

DIAMOND KITE

You need stiff cardboard, brightly colored tissue paper, glue, and string. If you are planning to decorate the kite, you will want sequins, ribbons, buttons, beads, feathers, and other such trimmings.

Cut out diamond shapes from the cardboard pieces. Now cut out two triangle shapes for the diamond for each kite. Cover both triangles with the tissue paper. Make a tiny hole at the top of the smaller triangle, and then thread the string through. Decorate the kite with the assorted decorations. Each guest can take his kite home to place on the wall.

★ *This is a decorative kite that is great for display or as a gift—but is not for flying!*

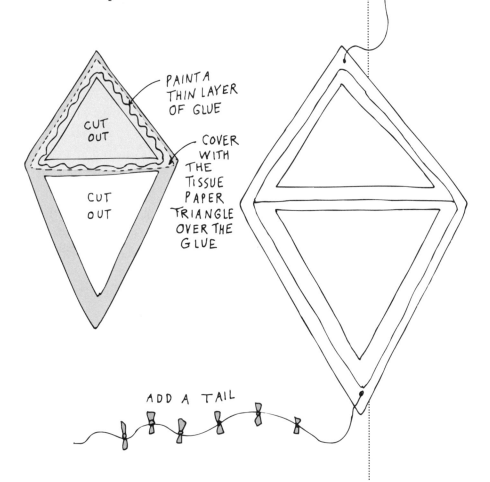

PAINT A THIN LAYER OF GLUE

CUT OUT

CUT OUT

COVER WITH THE TISSUE PAPER TRIANGLE OVER THE GLUE

ADD A TAIL

77

CHIMNEY
CUT
4
4"

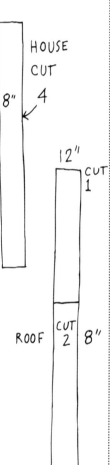

HOUSE
CUT
4
8"

12"
CUT
1

ROOF CUT 2 8"

HOME-BASE KITE

You will need scissors, glue, heavy cardboard, tissue paper, kite string (lightweight), and, for a tail, strips of satin ribbons or crepe paper in many colors.

Cut four small strips of heavy cardboard, all the same size—4 inches each—(these will be the chimney). Cut four more strips twice as long as the first ones—8 inches each—(these will be the house). Now cut three strips, one 12 inches and two 8 inches each—(these will be the roof).

Glue the chimney and house strips into squares, and then glue the roof strips into a triangle (A). Glue the roof to the house, close to one side. Glue the chimney to the peak of the roof (B).

Cut a strip of heavy cardboard that is long enough to extend from the top of the chimney to the frame for a brace (C). Place the kite on the table with the brace facing you. Now you can tie the end of the kite string to the brace where it crosses the top of the house (D). Squeeze a thin line of glue on all the strips of the frame. The brace strip should face you with the string behind it (E).

Now lay a piece of tissue paper over the glued frame, and press it flat. Trim the overlapping paper from the frame (F). Cut a piece of tissue paper as wide as the bottom of the house plus a little extra. Cut slits into one edge for a fringed tail. Glue the tail to the bottom of the kite (G).

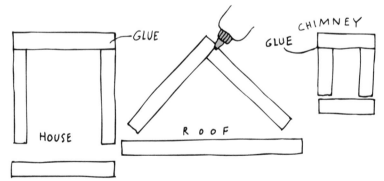

HOUSE

GLUE

ROOF

GLUE CHIMNEY

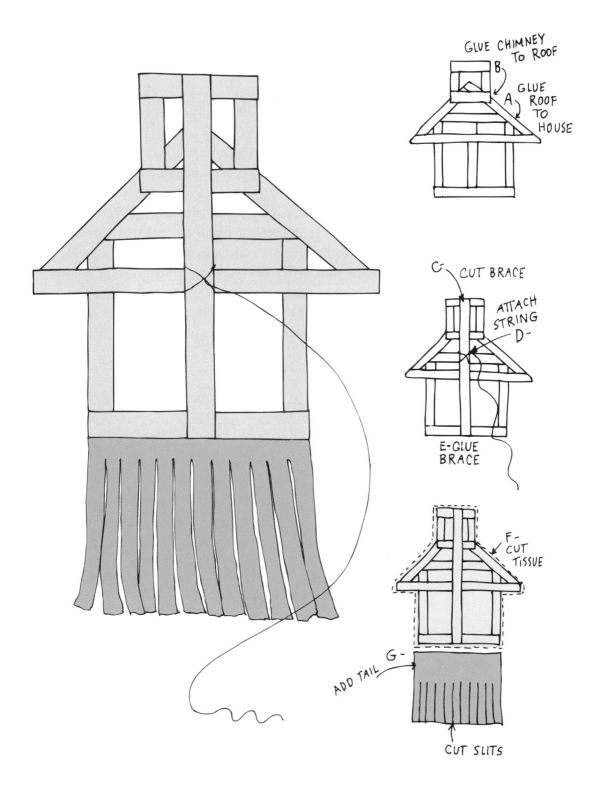

GLUE CHIMNEY TO ROOF

B

A — GLUE ROOF TO HOUSE

C — CUT BRACE

ATTACH STRING D —

E - GLUE BRACE

F — CUT TISSUE

ADD TAIL G —

CUT SLITS

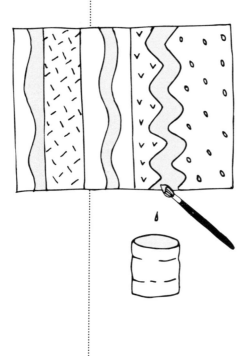

WIND SOCKS

For one per guest and a couple of spares to use "in case," you will need sheets cut up into strips (rectangles about 14 by 20 inches), ribbons cut into 18-inch lengths, fabric paint and paintbrushes, newspapers, metal coat hangers, wire cutters, pliers, scissors, heavy yarn, and an adult with some sewing skills.

Each guest can make his own wind sock. Before the party, precut the fabric and bend the wire hangers into circles (bend them around the top of a coffee can for easier shaping) for the tops of the wind socks so everything is ready for the guests to put together. Prepare a table for work by covering it with newspapers and placing on it a selection of paints in jars and paintbrushes. Provide water in other jars or soup cans for easy cleaning of the brushes.

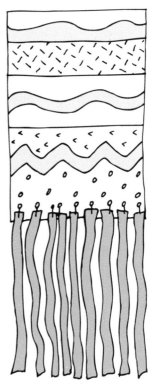

When the guests arrive, they can paint the strips of fabric in different colors and let them dry while they move on to other projects. When the fabric is dry, lay it out and arrange the ribbon streamers along the bottom of the sock (on the reverse, or wrong, side). Pin the streamers to the sock and then give the sock to the sewing specialist to sew them on. Seam the wind sock, but leave the seam out on the wrong side. Now fit the wire circle to the top of the sock, fold ⅝ inch of fabric over the wire, and then pin the folded fabric. Use a large hand stitch to create a hem with the wire inside. Now turn the sock right side out and add some heavy yarn at the top to form a hanger for the sock.

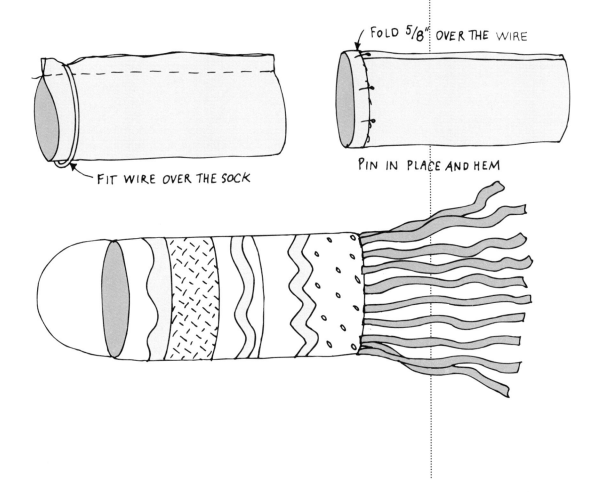

FOLD ⅝" OVER THE WIRE

FIT WIRE OVER THE SOCK

PIN IN PLACE AND HEM

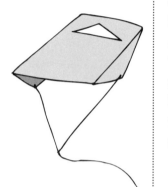

GARBAGE BAG KITE

For each kite, you will need a white plastic garbage bag about 23 by 29 inches, two dowels (about ¼ inch), tape, string, and some permanent markers in bright colors. To begin, spread each bag flat, and measure and mark the cutting lines as below. Cut along the lines (you will throw away the areas that are striped). Turn the kite over and tape the dowels in position. Use tape to reinforce the corners of the cutout and the wing tips. Poke a tiny hole in each wing tip, and tie one end of a 10-foot piece of string through each one. This is the kite's bridle. Tie a loop at the end of the bridle, and attach your flying line to this.

★ *If you can't spend the time making kites, or are concerned that your home-made kites won't fly as well, you can buy a variety of inexpensive kites that will be ready for flying.*

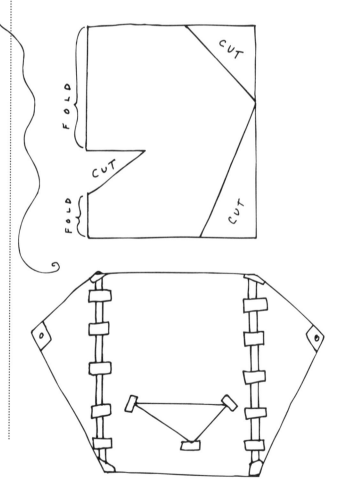

STREAMER KITES

For very young kids, gather lots of crepe paper streamers in different colors. Give each child about ten streamers to hold in his hand. Have him run around the yard, holding the streamers above his head to watch how the wind makes them fly. The kids can also tie the streamers to a tree or a stick and see them fly in the wind.

FLYING SAUCERS

There are many other flying objects that are lots of fun to fly on a day where there is little or no wind, or as another activity after the initial kite flying expedition. At your local toy store, you will find an assortment of Frisbees, Paradiscs, flying rings, boomerangs, aerobic footballs, plastic neon kites, and slingshots.

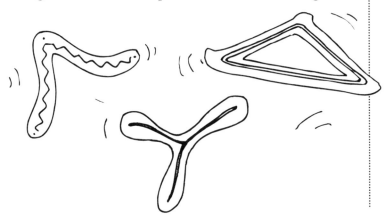

★ *DON'T TRY THIS AT HOME! Indonesian children love to fly kites, especially in the weeks before the rainy season in September, when the winds are very strong. The children choose bright new kites in the shapes of birds, butterflies, and dragons. The best kites are said to be on lines coated with crushed glass, because the object of the competitions is to cut loose the other players' kites. About ten competitors launch their kites together, and as their lines cross, kites break free and disappear into the sky. The person who is left flying the last kite wins the competition.*

83

FLYING FISH

Photocopy our flying fish and distribute copies to all your guests. Have guests decorate the fish. When finished, tie a string through the eye and attach to a chopstick.

MENU

KITE SANDWICHES

FRUIT KEBOBS

SNAPPIN' SALAD

POTATO SALAD

GRADUATION

DON'T NECESSARILY WAIT FOR THE BIG ONES (like high school or grade school graduations) for an occasion to celebrate with family and friends. This is a graduation party to give after your child completes *any* grade or special class. Completion of a grade or an after-school course like art, music, puppet making, or ballet can be reason enough for everyone to cheer!

★ *Our friend Stephanie Mintz loves miniature golf, so her dad, Ira, turned her back yard into a miniature golf course. He laid down scraps of wood to form paths to direct the balls around the course, and used old plastic pipe for connections. He made mud puddles, dirt hills, obstacles, and loops just by using his imagination and sand and water. Old doll-houses, miniature cars, gift boxes, pots and pans—all served as attractions at different holes in the course.*

Used golf balls were placed in a large plastic ice bucket that looked like a golf ball. And as the final touch, Ira borrowed old clubs and miniature pencils and pads from his local golf course.

INVITATION

Make a diploma: "This certifies that (name) has successfully completed 'Chess for Beginners.' A party honoring this achievement will be held at Roger Glazebrook's, 1 East End Avenue, New York, on April 4th at 6:00 pm. RSVP: 555-1234.

"Be sure to bring an old pair of sneakers for a surprise!"

Add a gold seal from the stationery store, insert in a large envelope, and mail.

DECORATIONS

Fill the room with balloons and streamers. Make a balloon arch by tying balloons along a ribbon or a string. Helium balloons will be easiest. You can also anchor the rope with strings attached from the arch to the ceiling or walls. The balloons can also be tacked around a doorjamb, creating an archway.

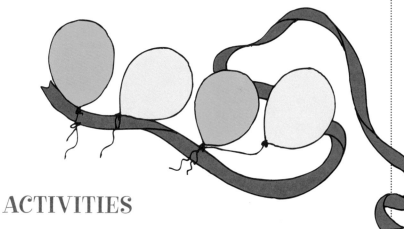

ACTIVITIES

TAKE A CLASS PICTURE

After all the guests have arrived, stage a class photo. If you have access to a one-hour photo developing shop, send someone (a teenage helper would be ideal) with the film to get a copy for each child to take home as a keepsake of the year and a favorite party favor.

★ *Chris Stevens purchased a "You Are Special" plate a few years ago and finds that she uses it for her four sons all the time. The ceramic hand-painted plate is used to serve the honoree's dinner or snack. Winning a tennis match, bringing home an A, and passing the driver's test have all been used as excuses to bring out the plate!*

★ *"Don't forget the elation young girls feel when 'flying up' from Brownie to full-fledged Girl Scout,"* says Cammy Blackstone. *"That's an excellent time to have a party."*

DECORATE YOUR SNEAKERS

Everyone will have brought an old pair of sneakers from the school year. Gather together marking pens, puff paints, glue, sequins, buttons, feathers, ribbons—anything you can think of. Let imagination take over as the guests "refurbish" their old sneakers into artworks. You provide new shoelaces—the wilder, the better—and the transformation will be complete.

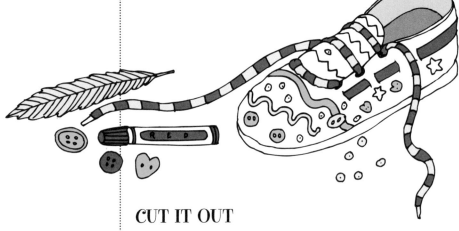

CUT IT OUT

Cut out pictures of animals from old magazines and calendars. Glue them to poster board or stiff paper. Cut each picture into several pieces. Give one piece of each animal picture to each guest and place the other parts on a table or floor. Players must search for the rest of their picture and put the puzzle together. The game becomes harder the more puzzle pieces there are, so you can control the degree of difficulty according to the age of the players.

JINGLE HANDKERCHIEF RELAY

Divide the players into two teams and line them up. Give the first member of each team a handkerchief with a small bell tied to one corner. That player shakes the bell three times, makes a complete turn in place, shakes the bell three more times, and passes the handkerchief to the player behind him. The procedure is repeated down the line to the last player. He then brings the handkerchief back to the first player, who shakes the bell five times. The first team to finish wins.

HIGH-TAIL IT

Guests line up holding each other around the waist. Place a handkerchief in the last player's back pocket or waistband so that most of it is hanging out. When play begins, the front of the line chases the end of the line trying to catch the handkerchief. The middle of the line controls the direction of play as they move in different directions. If someone lets go and the line breaks, he's out. If someone catches the handkerchief, he's "It" and goes to the back of the line.

★ *At Lee Berber's graduation party, decorations reminded everyone that applying to college was OVER! Tombstones made out of Styrofoam carried the names of colleges everywhere. Tables were covered in plastic cloths and napkins in the school colors, and had blue exam books in the center— friends were encouraged to write anecdotes about Lee on the inside pages. Flash cards of vocabulary words and college catalogues were strewn everywhere. And Lee's mother, as a surprise, had pictures of Lee's friends blown up, and glued to each picture was a bumper sticker from the college they would be attending!*

★ *When Stephanie Mintz graduated from high school, her mother Marcia decided to give her a Peter Pan going-away party, thinking that the kids might want to delay growing up just a little longer. Thus Steph's favorite childhood book served as the grand design as her home was turned into her very own Never-Never Land. Invitations were green felt hats, each with a feather glued to the top, with the words "I never want to grow up" written across the top with a black marker. Marcia blew up drawings from the book* Peter Pan, *on which she pasted photos of Steph's friends who were graduating. Guests danced under twinkling white Christmas lights in memory of Tinker Bell.*

LISTEN UP

This is an audio scavenger hunt. Divide the players into two teams in your own house and yard. Give each team a list of sounds they must find and record. You will need two tape recorders to collect sounds. The first team to complete the list wins. Prizes for the team can be noisemakers of some sort—whistles, horns, kazoos.

Examples of sound to record:

TICKING CLOCK
BIRD
SODA FIZZING
WATER DRIPPING
TOILET FLUSHING
CAR HORN
AIR CONDITIONER OR FURNACE
LAUGHTER
DOG BARKING

WHISTLE
RADIO NEWS
RINGING TELEPHONE
TELEPHONE BUSY SIGNAL
CAT PURRING
FAUCET DRIPPING
VACUUM CLEANER
DOORBELL

THE GRADUATION CEREMONY

Recognize each guest as he walks through the balloon arch. Hand each one something symbolic of the occasion—a diploma, a blue ribbon, or a trophy. You can treat the commencement seriously or youcan invent silly awards for these presentations.

FAVORS

Fancy shoelaces from which your guests choose to add extra style to their newfangled tennis shoes; diplomas; blue ribbons.

MENU

STAR PIZZAS

CLASS CUPCAKES

FRUIT POPS

CARAMEL MINI POPCORN BALLS

★ *Sam and Jake Sadle (ages nine and six) have a mom who believes in acknowledging the end of a school project that has been a struggle. She makes a fuss over the victorious student, allowing him to choose a special menu or pick a movie for the family to see. Commemorating even such everyday holidays is what this book is all about.*

GRAMPS THE GREATEST!

ALTHOUGH SEPTEMBER 8 IS THE INFORMALLY designated Grandparents' Day, these important family members can be celebrated any day. Whether it's Gramps or Gram or both, choose a time, proclaim the holiday, and start the preparations. The first step is to clear the date with the honorees. Plan for one person or a whole group. Spend the day, or a few days, getting ready for your party. There's no reason to fret over these plans. You'll seldom have more cooperative or appreciative guests!

INVITATION

The grandchildren should invite the guests of honor. Have your child choose a favorite painting or produce a new one. Create a frame by pasting the art on a piece of colored paper or a new photograph and write the invitation copy around the picture with a Magic Marker. Create a frame.

★ *You can ask the guests to bring a photo of themselves as babies. Hang these up around the room. Play a game where everyone has to guess who is who.*

DECORATIONS

Memorabilia make the best decorations for a celebration like this. Dust off the photos showing all family members that have been lying in a shoebox or stuck in a drawer, and display them everywhere you can think of—attached with magnets, lying flat on tables, tacked to bulletin boards. Get out the scrapbooks. Pick at least one family videotape to show. Think about constructing a family tree as part of the decor.

ACTIVITIES

GRANDMA'S ATTIC

Dress for the day should be the fashion at the time when your grandparents were young. Borrow appropriate accessories to carry out the theme.

TIME CAPSULES

Collect 3-pound coffee cans for as many kids as will be participating. Decorate with paint or fabric glue-on pictures, stickers, or other "found" objects. Does Grandma want to help? The cans are now ready to fill with pictures, drawings, mementos, family statistics, letters, cards, and other memorabilia useful for commemorating Grandparents' Day. Each year, start a new repository or simply add to the old ones. Why not include taped interviews with grandparents and special pictures of your Annual Grandparents' Day?

START A FAMILY HISTORY SCRAPBOOK

In the unlikely event that you don't already have a family album, it's not too late to begin! Find old photographs, souvenirs, and letters that have been preserved in your family. Use them to start your own scrapbook. Ask grandparents to help compile items and stories for your book. Set up an environment for the children to interview their grandparents—video cameras were made for times like this, but audiotape will produce good results as well. Ask for everyone's comments about the photos and letters, and add all the family history.

Another version of a time capsule is a kind of family tree. Make the capsule out of a large cardboard cylinder covered in aluminum foil. Together, choose things that should be included: charts of everyone's name, height, and weight; photographs; handwriting samples; drawings; written anecdotes. Ask family members to write short stories detailing what they did this past year. You can also include the front page of your local newspaper as well as the latest yearbook. Photocopies of diplomas and other important documents, postcards from family vacations, and special greeting cards are all perfect for the time capsule.

When you have included everything you have picked, tape the capsule shut. Label it with the day and year. Store it in a safe but secluded place. Next year, when you have another Grandparents' Day, you can open the old capsule and share the memories together.

★ *Joanie Donohue, a Pleasantville, New York, mom, keeps framed pictures of her parents as kids where her kids can look at them and enjoy the fact that their grandparents were actually kids once, too!*

★ *Annie's sister, Sonia Israel, together with a friend who was a graphic artist, drew a family tree on a 6-foot white sheet. On each of the branches they glued a picture of a member of the family. When done, the painting represented the history of the family and acted as a catalyst for the older generation to tell stories that fascinated the youngsters. You can use real branches and hang names and pictures of family members. Anchor the tree branches in pots of sand, or tape them to the wall.*

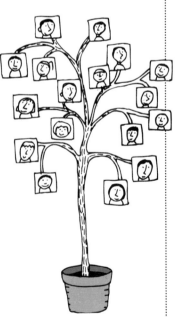

CHART YOUR FAMILY TREE

Older children can easily become fascinated with official genealogy charts of the generations of your family. Such records show relationships as far back as is known. They show where and when all members were born, where they lived, and when they moved and to what location. Go back through your family history to locate as much information as possible, searcing for anecdotal records as well. Stories, jokes and reminiscences all make this personal history even more interesting to kids. It's *your* tree and will reflect *your* family.

SPECIAL REPORT

Interview Grandma and Grandpa—make sure you have your tape recorder and/or a video camera. Preparing the questions you want to ask before the party will make your results much better. Ask the ordinary questions that come easily to mind (where and when were you born? maiden name?) but also look for topics that will reveal interesting information about the guests of honor and earlier times in which they lived. For example, "What was it like when you were younger? What games did you play? What did you get in trouble for? What jobs did you have? What would you change if you could? What is your funniest memory?"

THE NO COMPARISON GAME

Make a game out of an exercise that commonly takes place in many households. All ages can play, and it may even teach the kids something about "the good old days"! Gather a collection of foodstuffs and household items and guess the prices of the items fifty years ago. Be sure that current prices are known as well. If teams are competing, they should include all ages.

FUNNY FAMILY

Design a board game for your grandparents on their special day. Create a board and a deck of cards with family trivia questions written on them. Draw a trail with stops that have personal symbols attached to them. To play the game, have each player take turns rolling the dice, moving his marker according to the number on the dice, and picking a card according to what is indicated by the space on which he's landed. Every player needs a marker, which should be a small item belonging to the player such as a ring, a coin, a barrette, or a pin. Keep this simple by making a paper overlay on a game that your family is familiar with and likes to play. Design your board game around that one, substituting your family's stories for those in the commercial game. Cards might read as follows: Dad's birth date is June 5, 19??; Grandma's middle name is _____; Sister Sara's favorite color is _____. Advance to the next square with a right answer; go back a square if the answer is wrong. The first player to complete the trail wins.

★ *Celebrate Gramps (or Grams) the Greatest even if he or she lives too far away to be there. Send a journal with a description of what you did for the party. Buy a photo album and fill it with current pictures of everyone, plus drawings or some contribution from each family member.*

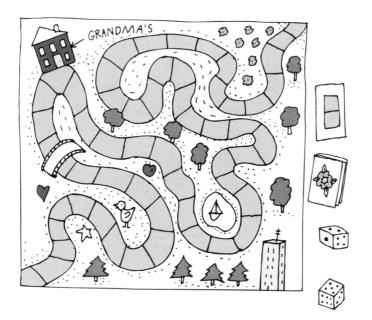

★ *For the menu: Base your menu on your grandparents' favorite childhood dishes (ask ahead of time). Or surprise them with a heritage dish that you make for them. Your family may have a "famous" recipe for spaghetti and meatballs, corned beef and cabbage, rice and beans, or matzo ball soup. Tailor the meal to your family.*

DESIGN A FAMILY CREST

Unless your family has traced its lineage to the highlands of Scotland or the interior regions of Japan, you probably are unaware of any design made especially for your family's clothing. These crests, which were readily identifiable, were sewn into clothing and made into flags throughout history. Think about what symbol or item could be used as a recognizable image of your family, and design your own crest. Does your last name have a meaning? Is there a particular line of work or hobby that people identify with your family? Maybe the grandparents or great-grandparents' country of origin could be worked into a design. Was it mountainous? Were there many wild animals and birds? Try doing this as a group project.

MENU

HORSERADISH MASHED POTATOES

CHICKEN VERA CRUZ

CARROT SOUFFLÉ

JUST DESSERTS

HAVE A HEART

CALL IT VALENTINE'S DAY IF YOU WANT, but don't eliminate other days of the year for hearts and flowers, Cupid, and friendship. If you choose a date other than the traditional February 14, just leave St. Valentine out of it and concentrate on the heart theme. There are times you want to pay special attention to a friend by celebrating a recent award or convalescence—or "just because." Send your hearts (elaborately presented or not) to your guest list, and start preparing.

INVITATION

These invitations are all kid-produced, so the design and degree of decoration are variable. First, choose the envelope size, then cut the heart to fit (that way you won't have to fold a heart). Make a heart template so you can cut as many hearts out of red paper as you need. Or try Janice Gilbar Treadwell's elaborate heart presentation, which is famous around Lyme, New Hampshire.

Janice uses doilies in all sizes and colors, construction paper, lace, artificial flowers, ¼-inch-wide satin ribbon, and pictures of cherubs, hearts, and other motifs all cut out from old valentines. Take a doily heart (in white, silver, or gold) and place a larger cut-out heart made from lace (a different color from the doily, preferably a vibrant shade of pink or purple) on it so there is a border around the doily. Glue down. Place this double heart on another, even larger paper cut-out heart, so there is another border around the double doily/lace heart. Now cut out cherubs and angels from other greeting cards or wrapping paper, and glue them around the edges of the larger paper heart (not the doily). Add some miniature silk roses (they come about a dozen to a bag at fabric stores) by gluing them randomly onto the doily. Take a satin ribbon about ¼ inch wide, fold it over, and glue it to one side of the invitation. From this, hang another small heart (this one can be made out of paper or can be a miniature stuffed heart that you can buy at fabric and party stores), which contains the actual invitation copy.

you are invited to
the LYNCHES'
Have a Heart
PARTY
♡ Feb. 14 ♡
at 6:00
555-1234
R·S·V·P

★ *Carole Ference has two daughters, now grown. When the girls were little, and even in their late teens, they found tiny candy hearts from Mom with messages on them on their pillows every Valentine's Day eve.*

DECORATIONS

Decorate with hearts everywhere. Long, skinny balloons twisted into abstract shapes also create a very festive atmosphere.

★ *Annie and Gary once gave a Valentine's Day party at a local diner. They covered the ceiling with nearly a thousand red, pink, purple, and silver balloons tied with colored streamers that they, with the help of several good friends, blew up using a rented helium tank. The effect of the ceiling totally covered in balloons was magical and set the tone for the entire evening. Using balloons to decorate a large space is relatively inexpensive. Of course, around February 14, a "Happy Valentine's Day" banner with large bows at each end is also appropriately decorative.*

ACTIVITIES

HEART HUNT (OR "HAVE A HEART")

Buy pastel candy hearts with sayings on them. Hide the hearts around the house. Players get one point for green, two points for pink, etc., and get bonus points for matching heart.

THAT'S AMORE

Have everyone sit in a circle and tell a story, each guest saying only one sentence. Try to make the story unusual, funny, and surprising. Keep going, with everyone getting more than one chance to change the direction of the story so that no one knows where it is going. Be sure to tape the story and play it back to the guests at the party.

HEARTS

Make a large heart on the floor using 6 feet of string. Each player takes turns attempting to throw a bean bag into the heart from 10 feet away. Give everyone three tries; the player with the most successes wins.

"FULL OF BEANS" HEARTS

This is a craft project for young kids to make and take home as a favor. Prepared some cut-out red and pink felt hearts ahead of time, using our template. Punch holes according to the drawing. With large needles and colored yarn, sew two small hearts together and fill with dried beans. Finish the ends by tying a knot. Be sure to have an adult check the security of the sewing. The finished project should be a bean bag for playing "hearts" (see opposite page) and for taking home as a memento.

If the kids are very young, you can sew the hearts together the day before and have the kids fill them at the party.

HEART ON A STRING

Red, white, and pink Sculpey clay will make hard-to-beat heart necklaces. Let your guests make hearts from the clay and punch holes in them with toothpicks. Bake according to the directions on the package. When the hearts dry, string them onto a piece of colored yarn. For a variation, make beads with a heart pendant.

★ *Lisa Simpson, growing up in Philadelphia, always dropped off anonymous valentines throughout the neighborhood. Each said, "Happy Valentine's Day from all your neighbors!" No one ever knew that it was Lisa who was the good neighbor fairy—but they all talked about that secret valentine and how great it made them feel!*

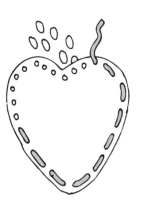

103

★ *Nelle Niles (that's her real name) had four daughters and one son. All through their childhoods, at every Valentine's Day, Nelle bought several little gifts for each child, wrapped them up in elaborate papers and ribbons, and wrote loving cards on it. The kids always felt that this holiday was not only for older lovers but also for the love between parents and children.*

PICTURE FRAMES AND JEWELRY MAKING WITH BEADS

By buying some bags of assorted beads at a party supply or bead shop, you'll have all the tools the guests will need.

★ Give each guest a Plexiglas frame, plastic beads, and glue in a tube. Each can glue the beads around the perimeter of the frame, and then build a three-dimensional design by continuing to glue the beads on top of one another.

★ Buy some heart buttons at your local fabric store; the children string them on elastic to make a bracelet or a necklace.

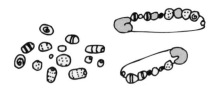

★ String plastic beads of different sizes and colors onto large safety pins to create decorative pins quickly and easily.

PLACE MATS

Weaving heart-shaped place mats is another perfect activity for young kids. Cut out 12-inch-long, 1-inch-wide strips of red, white, and pink construction paper. Help the children weave strips into place mats (see the drawing), and then cut each place mat into a heart shape using a stencil as a guide.

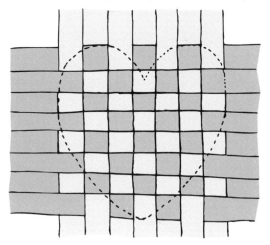

FIND YOUR MATCH

Cut hearts in half, making each cut a little different from the others, and pin a half heart on each guest's sleeve. Then each guest has to find his partner—or you can place the matching heart half on the table and have each guest find his seat by matching the heart on his sleeve.

For a variation, write words associated with hearts on each paper heart, such as *beating, stolen, sweet, broken, burning, heavy, faint, soft, hard, cold, brave,* or *lion hearts.*

VALENTINE'S MASK

Emotions are triggered by music. Play music selections and act out the feelings they evoke: silly, funny, happy, sick, sleepy, angry, sad—you interpret the music and emotions by moving your body.

★ *You can write each word on a whole heart and then cut the heart in half so guests have to match half-words to make a whole.*

★ *Hilda and Mike Petruncola, from New Fairfield, Connecticut, celebrated Valentine's Day as a family holiday. They divided up the Valentine's Day chores. Dad Mike was in charge of getting gifts and cards for the girls, Roseann and Chrisann, and Mom Hilda was in charge of Michael, Donald, and Paul (one year they all got red socks).*

EDIBLE PLACE CARDS

Take graham crackers and use white icing to glue red candy hearts in each corner. Write a guest's name on the front and put a cracker at each place setting.

COOKIE DECORATING

After you have made the heart cookie pops, the kids can decorate them at the party and eat them for dessert. They also make great favors.

MENU

CRANBERRY PUNCH WITH HEART ICE MOLD

HEART SANDWICHES

STRAWBERRY DIVINE

COOKIE POPS

HIT THE ROAD

IS THERE AN ADULT OUT THERE who doesn't remember the day he or she got a driver's license? Marsha Mintz's daughter Michelle's birthday was in January, so she was the first on her block in Los Angeles to get her license. That was indeed a cause for great celebration, and since all of Michelle's friends were obsessed with driving and with obtaining that magical license, Michelle and Marsha decided to give a "Finally, I'm Driving Party" for her sixteenth birthday. You will see that what's amazing about this party is the unforgettable atmosphere created.

INVITATION

A driver's license with a colored picture on it. Take your state driver's license and make one colored photocopy of it. Marsha took a picture of Michelle's face, cut it out, and glued it right on the photocopied driver's license.

On a computer or typewriter, write out the words "LICENSE TO INVITE EVERYONE TO HIT THE ROAD." Photocopy as many invitations as you need. Take them to your local copy shop and have them laminated. (You can laminate eight on one sheet.)

For the RSVP card, pick up a copy of a permit test at the local Department of Motor Vehicles, photocopy the front and back of the DMV test, cut out sections of eight questions at a time, white out two of those questions, and with a typewriter, type in your own questions and answers. On the back of each return piece, draw seven boxes side by side, and write "Choose your own vanity plate." Thus, each invitee is asked to write in the letters for his or her favorite vanity plate. That gets sent with the RSVP card.

★ *For a variation, Marsha suggests including a key chain with paper or metal keys hanging in the envelope. These can be party favors.*

At your local automobile club you will find stickers of all kinds to decorate the invitation envelope. Marsha picked up "buckle up for safety" stickers and automobile club stickers.

★ *Place cards: Use the vanity plates that the guests chose on their RSVP cards. . It's a lot of fun to watch the guests not only try to find their own vanity plates but read everybody else's. You can buy little "name" license plates at notion and party stores.*

★ *You can blow up the Driver's License to hang as a poster.*

DECORATIONS

Go to your local auto club and pick up various road maps from all over the country. Use them as tablecloths for your tables. If you can, remove all your furniture from your living room and dining room or family room and turn these rooms into a large parking lot and a gas station. At AAA Flag & Banner in Los Angeles, you can order 16-foot-long banners or plastic colored triangle flags, and hang them back and forth across the room from the ceiling. Using colored masking tape, tape lengths on the floor to make parking spaces. Rent 6-foot folding tables and plan to seat six to eight people at each: four on one side and one or two at either end, leaving the other 6-foot side empty. Cover each table with the maps. Marsha's brother-in-law, Robert Gunther, copied outlines of cars on 8-foot pieces of foam board and then cut along the outlines to make a VW bug, a Corvette, a Jeep, a station wagon, and other models.

★ *Michelle's cousin wore a rented orange hazard jacket. Holding a flashlight, he handed each guest one hubcap and a paper plate that fit into the center of the hubcap. This all took place in the "parking lot"—the family room or dining room, which became a gas station.*

★ *Make a poster of traffic lights to hang around the room. You can also put red, green, and yellow lightbulbs into existing lamps.*

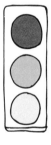

Tape one car per table lengthwise against the 6-foot side of the table where no one will be seated. When the guests sit at the other three sides, it looks as if they're sitting in the car. Remember those permit tests you cut up for the RSVP card? Get more of them and glue one whole test at each place setting. Place a pen at each place setting. At the top of each place setting, put a booklet on learning to drive (Marsha added a booklet on drinking and driving from the Auto Club).

There are several varieties of paper plates with cars and/or gas pumps on them. You can also rent hubcaps at your local auto supply store. These will probably be used hub caps, so you'll have to wash them. They are used as serving trays for guests.

In one corner of this second room, place a round serving table and tape a car to it, just as you did with the cars in the other room, and a foam-board gas tank painted with the name of your favorite gas and SELF SERVE. You can tape a rubber hose to the other side with a glue gun, making it look more like a gas tank. On the center of this self-serve table, place a clean

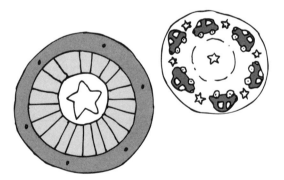

tire flat. In the middle of the tire, place a large salad bowl filled with lettuce. Around the table, in smaller hubcaps, place dishes each with a different salad fixing inside: mushrooms, green onions, sprouts, tomatoes, peppers, cucumbers, carrots, garbanzo beans. Your guests, carrying their hubcaps with paper plates inside, walk around the self-serve gas tank and help themselves to salad.

The next table is a gas tank that says FULL SERVE. For this gas tank, Marsha hired some teenagers who wore gas station uniforms borrowed from the local gas station. These kids made sandwiches and served them.

CENTERPIECES

In the center of each table, place a Styrofoam square painted yellow and black to resemble a warning sign. You can also make other signs, such as RR for railroad, YIELD, and a red STOP sign.

ACTIVITIES

VIDEO & OTHER GAMES FOR OLDER KIDS

Play video racing games on Nintendo or computer.

DANCING

Since these kids are sixteen years old, dancing is the prime activity. Gather your favorite CDs or tapes, and blast the music.

★ *Michelle's grandfather, Bernie Mintz, rented a police uniform from a local costume shop. The Mintzes also rented sawhorse barricades, orange cones, and road signs (DETOUR, STOP, SLOW, YIELD). As each car drove up and parents dropped off their kids, Grandpa Bernie handed each a little traffic ticket. Each traffic ticket had the guest's name on it and instructions about what car table to sit at and where to look for the personalized vanity plate.*

THANK-YOU NOTES

Marsha took a picture of each table of guests and then duplicated the film so that she would have one picture per guest per table. Michelle wrote her thank-you note on the back of each picture. (Each guest got both a thank-you note and a picture of the party.)

★ You can also include a tiny flashlight, Band-Aids, maps, and so on.

FAVORS

Buy inexpensive clear plastic makeup bags at the dime store or drugstore. Use a permanent marker to write "Emergency Road Kit" on each. In each bag place a ballpoint pen, a small notebook, transparent tape, a little comb, a Band-Aid, a battery, and a plastic coin holder for holding change for meters.

MENU

SALAD BAR WITH VARIED DRESSINGS

BREAD WITH SEASONED BUTTERS; SPREAD OF LUNCH MEATS, CHEESES, AND GRILLED VEGETABLES

BANANA SPLIT HEAVEN

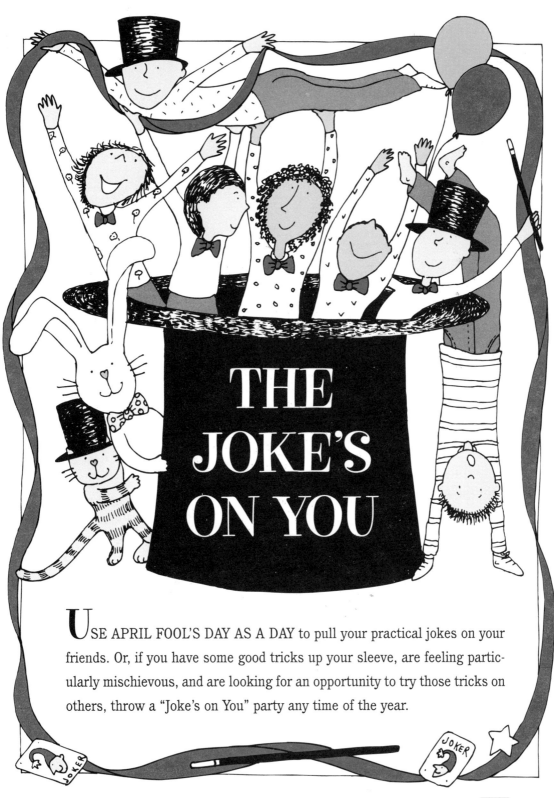

THE JOKE'S ON YOU

USE APRIL FOOL'S DAY AS A DAY to pull your practical jokes on your friends. Or, if you have some good tricks up your sleeve, are feeling particularly mischievous, and are looking for an opportunity to try those tricks on others, throw a "Joke's on You" party any time of the year.

★ *H. Allen Smith's* Book of Practical Jokes *will be of great inspiration to you and your guests for lots of silly fun.*

INVITATION

Photocopy the invitation below. Now make a slit in the hat with scissors or a knife. Fold over the hands so they look like they are clasping the front of the invitation. One hand has the flowers, the other slips right into the slit in the hat. When you open the invitation, the flowers will then pop out of the hat!

BACK

Where ignorance is bliss,
it's folly to be wise.
So come out to our party
in an April Fool's disguise.
We'll be goofy and silly
and may be in a fix,
on April the First
please arrive around six.

MAKE SLIT

P.S. BRING A TRICK

FRONT

DECORATIONS

★ On the front door, post a sign that says "We've been called out of town unexpectedly. For more information, please go around to the back door."

★ Put signs along the path to the back door (buy signs available at stationery stores: "No Spitting," "Llama Crossing," "For Sale," "Checks Cashed Here," "Baby On Board"—they will be appropriately silly used along the back yard path).

★ Place chairs upside down and facing the wall, turn vases over, hang mirrors askew, turn pictures backward.

★ In order to enter the back door at the beginning of the party, each guest must present a trick or tell a joke.

★ *Ask everyone to wear their clothes inside out and backward and to bring a joke or a trick. Then have a contest judging the best of each.*

ACTIVITIES

TRICK SHOW

To allow everyone to see the different tricks that the guests brought, have guests perform their tricks again in front of the whole crowd.

FOOL'S GOLD

In this scavenger hunt, players search for "Fool's Gold." Divide guests into teams. Give each team one hour to return with as many things on the list as they can. Marc and his friend Amos Buhai are the champs of the scavenger hunt in their crowd. They suggest these items for a good hunt:

a joker card, a baton, a mole, ties that bind, a wild hare, peas in a pod, a ghostwriter, a sign of the times, seed money, a lifeline, tears of a clown, a red nail, a bell bottom, a mark of excellence, square knot, flower power, food for thought, a hook, a rolling stone, travel plans, a flying saucer, braces, a single, a good-luck charm .

BLINDMAN'S BUFF

Every guest except one is blindfolded. The one who can see is "It" and has to stay out of the way of the blindfolded guests, who roam around attempting to catch the player who is "It." If the blindfolded guests touch someone, they ask, "Blindfolded?" If the answer is "Yes," then the "captured" player is released. Play continues until a blindfolded player touches the player who is not blindfolded, who then becomes "It."

MAGIC MOMENTS

Have a magician come to the party, or set aside some time for your guests to show the tricks they've brought to the party as instructed by the invitation. Annie once invited an aspiring high-school magician to demonstrate a few tricks in his repertoire for Marc's third birthday. When Marc turned thirteen, he and his friend Jeremy Konner did their magic tricks for Isabel Kaplan's third birthday. Because Marc and Jeremy were also kids, they did not scare the young girls, who thought the boys were "just the best!"

MENU

SUCKER FOOD:
EAT EVERYTHING WITH YOUR HANDS

SPAGHETTI PIE

AMBROSIA

CRAZY CUPCAKES

★ *"Sucker Food"—serve the cupcakes first, and insist that guests eat them with a knife and fork. Eat the spaghetti with a small plastic toy shovel.*

117

LOOK, IT'S SNOWING!

WAVES OF EXCITEMENT USUALLY ACCOMPANY the first snowflakes of the season. It's a great time to gather some neighborhood friends and celebrate. "Spontaneity" is the key word. There's a big advantage to snow parties: There are no ants, spiders, mosquitoes, or bees. A telephone call will suffice in planning a party. You'll have a fairly accurate fix on the weather when inviting guests while the snow is falling. Just call everyone and ask them to wear outdoor clothing. If you know your guests have sleds, ask them to bring their own.

ACTIVITIES

Begin by making snowmen and other snow figures. Keep everyone moving. If you have the facilities, you can go sledding and throw snowballs. Here are some of the best games to play to keep everyone warm!

ESKIMO JUMPING RACE

Line up all guests at a starting place. Have them fold their arms across their chests, knees rigid and feet close together. Jump forward in short jumps. The course may be as long as you choose.

FOX AND GEESE

Mark a large circle (15 to 30 feet in diameter) in the snow. Cross the circle with lines like spokes in a wheel. Divide the guests into two teams: foxes and geese. The geese disperse around the rim of the wheel and one goose in each den or area between the spokes. A fox stands in the center of the wheel. As the fox runs after the geese to tag them, the geese run along the spokes or rim of the wheel to another den, where they are safe. Players may not run outside the wheel. When a goose is tagged, he becomes the fox.

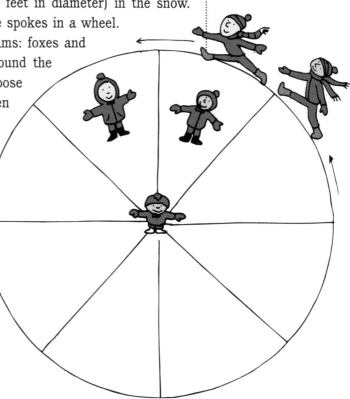

★ *Beverly Maxwell's three grown children remember their family tradition of cutting the Christmas tree more than Christmas itself. Each year, two or three other families would join them as they selected trees outside of Bellevue, Washington, to cut. The day always included a cold-weather picnic lunch of chili, hot chocolate, and apple cider and the singing of carols.*

★ *If snow is not sufficiently wet, you can moisten it with a little water to make it stick when building.*

★ *The Snow Sculpture Contest can be done in teams.*

★ *Be prepared for all your guests to come in with wet boots and wet coats. Spread old rugs and towels on the floor in advance.*

SNOW CRAB RACE

Divide guests into teams (the number of teams will depend on the number of sleds you have available). Each racer lies on his stomach on a sled. Set the goal line. At a given signal the contestants push the sleds forward with their hands. No contestant may use his feet to make the sled go forward. The flatter the terrain, the better!

SNOW SCULPTURE CONTEST

Time contestants to see who can make a sculpture the fastest. Or give awards for the biggest, most creative, longest, or highest.

SNOWMAN DRESSING CONTEST

Provide props for your guests to dress the snowmen: old scarves, hats, glasses, shoes, jewelry. Give prizes for the funniest or the most elegant.

SNOW PAINTING

Gather old spray bottles, clean them out carefully, and fill them with water. Add a different shade of food coloring to each bottle. Let guests share bottles as they create a mural together or make individual paintings on the snow.

SNOW ON BLACK PAPER AND MAGNIFYING GLASS

Capture snowflakes on a sheet of cold black paper and examine them, using a magnifying glass. Are any two snowflakes the same?

★ *Clothespins will keep mittens in pairs.*

INSIDE: MAKE SNOWFLAKES

A great activity for young kids: Fan-fold a sheet of white paper. Cut out shapes and slits to make a snowflake. Unfold and check out your snowflake.

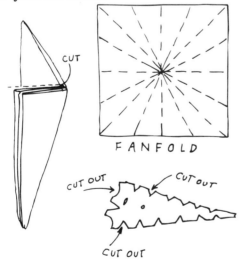

CUT

FANFOLD

CUT OUT   CUT OUT

CUT OUT

★ *In the marshmallow snowmen, you can use the string licorice instead of toothpicks and then everything is edible.*

SNOW SPELL

Using alphabet macaroni letters from your pantry, spell words such as *snow, icicle, frost,* and *sled*. Divide the players into two teams; the team with the most words wins. Or, for a variation, time individuals as they spell the longest word they can.

MARSHMALLOW SNOWMEN WITH TWIGS

Each guest will need three marshmallows and a few toothpicks. Stick one marshmallow on a toothpick for a head and use another marshamallow for a body. Cut the third marshmallow in half for arms. Cloves may be inserted for eyes, and a small twig stuck in an "arm" can be the snowman's broom.

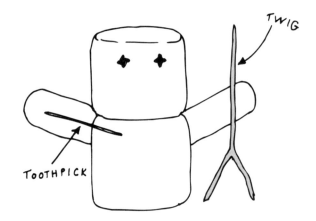

MENU

SNOW CONES

TRIPLE CHICKEN NOODLE SOUP

SNOWBALLS

HOT COCOA WITH MINIATURE MARSHMALLOWS

★ *For a delicious treat, try our SNOW PUDDING recipe which can be found in* The Penny Whistle Christmas Party Book *on page 114.*

MASK-ERADE

HALLOWEEN AND MARDI GRAS ARE THE "OFFICIAL" DAYS for disguises in this country. Most children, however, need no excuse for a full-blown dress-up day or costume occasion. They'll think it's a great idea, no matter what the calendar date. So without any excuses, let their imaginations soar with the creation of masks that will give them new personalities or decorate the walls of their rooms.

INVITATION

A mask—take simple face masks and decorate them. Each can be different, which makes it more fun to create. Ask the guests to bring the masks with them to the party.

This is a costume party—ask everyone to dress up in a disguise so they are not recognizable!

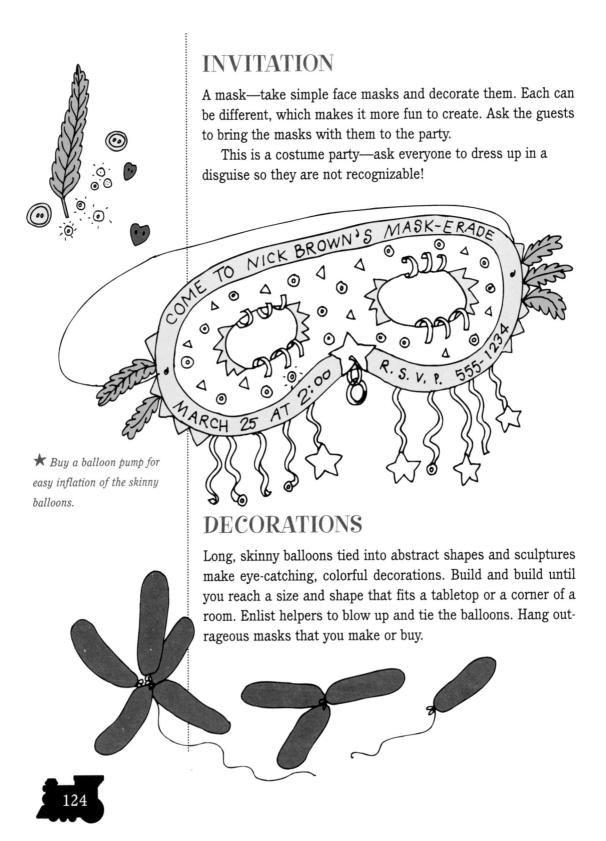

★ *Buy a balloon pump for easy inflation of the skinny balloons.*

DECORATIONS

Long, skinny balloons tied into abstract shapes and sculptures make eye-catching, colorful decorations. Build and build until you reach a size and shape that fits a tabletop or a corner of a room. Enlist helpers to blow up and tie the balloons. Hang outrageous masks that you make or buy.

ACTIVITIES

PRIZES

Award prizes for costume categories—most original, funniest, silliest, most beautiful, and so on. The biggest prize should go to the person no one recognized!

Buy some tapes of Brazilian carnival music (sambas are the best). Have them playing to get your guests into the celebrating mood.

PAPIER-MÂCHÉ MASKS

To make papier-mâché paste, stir together 1½ cups of flour with 3 cups of cold water. Pour into a small pot and simmer, stirring constantly with a wooden spoon, until the mixture has formed into a creamy paste. Add more water if the mixture gets too thick. Let cool.

To make a simple mask, spread petroleum jelly over the inside bottom and inside sides of a metal pie pan. Cut newspaper into strips and dip them into the papier-mâché paste. When you have covered the pan with one layer of paper dipped into the papier-mâché paste, make another layer over the first one.

To make the different parts of the face of the mask, use your imagination. You can make eyes out of buttons, ears out of cut-up egg cartons, noses out of clothespins or spools. Place the features on the mask and cover them with more strips that have been dipped into the papier-mâché. When the face mask is finished, the covered shapes will look like abstract bumps.

The mask now has to dry. Your guests may have to take them home to dry, unless it is a very hot day and you place them outside. When dry, they can be painted with acrylic paints. If you like, you can make them in advance and let the kids decorate them at the party.

★ *Hardware stores are perfect places to look for unusual decorations for your masks. Look through bins of old keys, screws, plates, and other paraphernalia for some hidden gems that will make your mask unusual and unforgettable.*

REALITY MASKS

This mask is appropriate for children aged eight and up. It is somewhat complicated, but the results are worth the effort! Be sure to have an adult supervising this activity. You will need plaster-of-paris bandages (the wider, the better), colored markers, petroleum jelly, scissors, newspaper, plastic sandwich wrap, acrylic paint, and decorations.

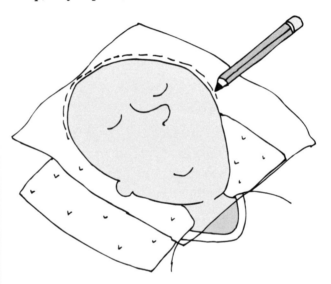

What makes these masks different is that they are made from patterns of each guest's face. Using tracing paper, hold the paper to the face and draw the outline of the face. Outline the eyes and nose with markers. Cut the pattern in half horizontally, just under the tip of the nose (the top half of the pattern will be from the hairline to the tip of the nose; the bottom half will be from the base of the nose, under the nostrils, to the bottom of the chin). Use this pattern to cut out the bandage pieces, two for the top and two for the bottom.

When ready, cover the guests' hair with plastic sandwich wrap and their faces with petroleum jelly. The adult now dips a piece of the bandage in water and then smooths it over the face. Add a bottom piece and then the two strips that connect the top and the bottom, down the center of the nose between the nostrils. Put the last two pieces on and smooth and mold the lips, eyes, and the nose and chin. The quick-drying bandage will set in about 3 minutes. Now remove the whole thing and paint and decorate.

HAND PAINTING

This is a festive way to get into the spirit of disguise. Use cheap liquid eyeliner—purple, green, blue, black, brown—to paint spiral designs on hands.

★ *Eleven-year-old Vivian Auld and her younger twin sisters, Alex and Wynne, have had lots of fun creating what they call "Masquerade Café." This homemade restaurant serves only important diners (like Mom and Dad). They spend hours preparing menus, decorating the dining room table, draping the windows to create a more romantic atmosphere, and finding the right waitress outfits. Their printed menus have a few items (like scrambled eggs and toast) that they are actually able to prepare and several fancier items (like frogs' legs risotto) that they claim to be out of, if they are ordered. After dinner, entertainment by the three Auld girls is an expected part of this unique family celebration.*

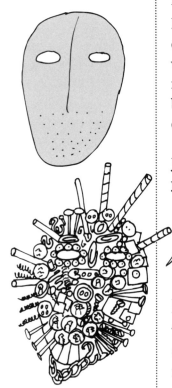

HOCKEY MASKS

In a sporting goods store, buy plastic hockey masks (they are called "goalie" face masks). Dip the entire mask into a plate of white glue. Now, using your wildest imagination, cover the mask with all kinds of objects—the more unlikely, the better: buttons, old pennies, sequins, beads (clay and plastic), paper clips, tiny rocks. Let dry.

You can also make a stunning futuristic mask very simply. Just totally cover the goalie mask with aluminum foil until all you see is a silver creature from outer space!

MINI MASKS

Take a square piece of colored paper, 3 inches square. Draw the eyes along the top edge and a big mouth near the bottom; for a nose, draw a circle so that you can fit this mini mask securely on your nose. Now decorate the mask with puff paints, sequins, feathers, glitter, or anything else you desire.

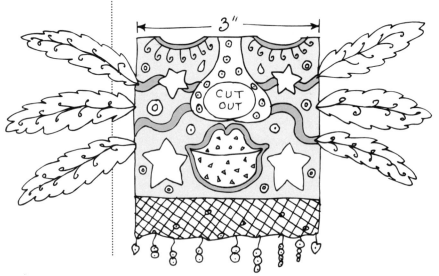

PAPER PLATE MASKS

These are favorites for young kids to make. Take any paper plates (the colored ones are perfect) and cut out holes for the eyes, nose, and mouth. You can color the mask or glue "found" objects all over it. When the mask is finished, glue it to a stick so a child can hold the mask by the stick and march around holding the mask in front of his face. This is a particularly great mask for a youngster who may not like wearing a mask and may feel more comfortable with one held in front of his face.

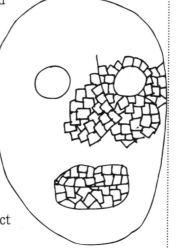

MOSAICS

Draw a face on a piece of cardboard that has some give to it. Cut out the outline and the eyes—this is now a mask. Gather colorful pages from magazines and cut out pieces of paper that you can glue over the mask in a mosaic-like pattern. (Don't draw a mosaic on the mask first and then try to fit pieces of paper into the lines—it is too difficult and frustrating. It is much easier to make your own abstract mosaic on your face drawing.)

★ *You can buy colored stickers in the shape of squares, circles, and rectangles at all stationery stores and use them to form a mosaic instead of cutting pieces out of magazines.*

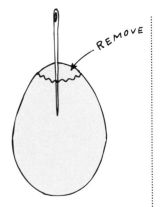

REMOVE

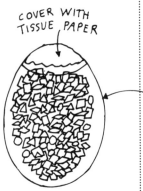

COVER WITH
TISSUE PAPER

FILL
WITH
CONFETTI

CRACKERS

For a confetti-filled treat, you'll need an egg, a needle, scissors, and confetti. Using a needle, punch a hole in one end of the egg. With scissors, enlarge the opening to the size of a quarter. Blow out the egg for cooking and wash the shell, leaving it to dry. Fill the shell with confetti (either purchase it at a party store or make your own by using a hole punch and construction paper in different colors). Glue a circle of tissue paper over the opening to hold the confetti. Decorate the egg with markers, glitter, and puff paints. When it's time to celebrate, remove the cap and shake out the confetti.

DECORATE

MENU

CHURASSCO

COUSCOUS

TOMATO SALAD

CHOCOLATE BANANAS

PLAY BALL

THE WORDS "PLAY BALL!" WARM ALL OUR HEARTS, and never more so when they mark the beginning of a new sports season. To commemorate the opening of any season—basketball, soccer, baseball—organize a game! Whether you plan it ahead of time or just organize a spur-of-the-moment get-together, first play the game you love, and then participate in the other activities we have included to round out your celebration.

INVITATION

Make your own pennant from felt and a little dowel, and use fabric paint in tubes to write your own invitation on it.

DECORATIONS

Get plastic statues for awards and ribbons for all the games, making sure everyone gets at least one for some activity. Divide your guest list in two and get bandannas in two colors that guests will wear to differentiate the teams.

ACTIVITIES

Organize a game of the sport you are celebrating. When that game is over, use some of these suggestions for quieter activities.

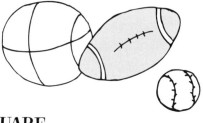 

FOUR SQUARE

Draw a square 6 by 6 feet with chalk on asphalt. Divide this square into four squares measuring 3 by 3 feet. Each of four players takes a spot in a square. Players decide who serves first. A player bounces a four-square ball and bats it with his hand into one of the other three squares. The player standing in that square must hit the ball into another square. Play continues until someone misses getting the ball within the lines of a square and thus receives a point. The first player to get ten points is out (and other players are eliminated as they each reach ten points). The last player is the winner.

★ Four-square balls are classic inflatable playground balls, 10 to 12 inches in diameter and made of hard rubber. They are available at sporting goods stores.

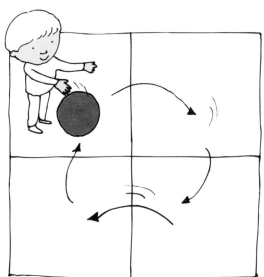

133

★ *Seastrom Associates (133 West 19th Street, New York, NY 10011; 212-243-1488) makes personalized baseball cards with a child's picture and statistics on the back. Send them a photo—preferably a head shot. Delivery takes five to six weeks.*

PIG PING-PONG

Set up a Ping-Pong table. Divide the guests into two teams, and line up the teams on opposite sides of the table. The first player on one team serves and passes the paddle to the next player in line. Meanwhile, the first player on the other side of the table must return serve and pass the paddle to the next player. The second player must return the serve and pass the paddle before the second player on the other side returns the hit. The relay continues until a side misses the ball or does not make the pass in time. The side that misses then gets a "P." Play continues until one team has spelled the word PIG, and the other team wins.

RECORD RELAY

Set up two rows of plastic jugs filled with water. Place the jugs about 5 feet apart, and set a starting line. Divide guests into teams behind the starting line. Give a ball to the first member of each team. At "GO," the first player from each team uses his feet to weave the ball around the jugs and then returns to the team, returning by the same route and passing the ball to the next player in line. The winning team is the one whose members complete the relay first.

THREE DROPS AND YOU'RE OUT

Form the players into two equal lines, facing each other, starting at about 5 feet apart. Throw the ball back and forth three times; then each line backs up 5 feet. Throw the ball back and forth three times and go back another 5 feet. You need one ball per team, per two people or alternately one ball per team taking turns à la relay line. If a player doesn't catch the ball, his team is out (or you might want to give everyone three outs).

For a variation, try throwing different sizes and kinds of balls at different lengths. You can even use beach balls, Ping-Pong balls, basketballs, soccer balls, or four-square balls.

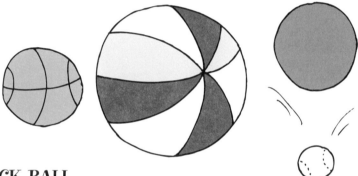

KICK BALL

Position four bases in the field as you would for baseball. Divide players into two teams. Use a four-square ball, or a beach ball for younger kids. One team is up; the other is in the field. The field must take positions of pitcher, catcher, at each base, and in the outfield. The pitcher rolls the ball to the first player "at bat," who must kick the ball. Just as in baseball, if it's a hit, the player runs to first base and must decide whether to try to go farther or remain safe. If the ball is caught in midair or the runner is tagged, he's out. Players continue to come to "bat" until three outs are made by the team in the field. Then the teams switch sides. Play continues for nine innings. The team with the most runs wins.

★ *In the Jansen house, Yankee opening day is a ritual. Mike and Tommy wear their new Yankee caps and jackets, take pictures, watch the game, and eat shelled peanuts, hot dogs, and popcorn. It's Mike's day to tell his son the stories of other opening days, show him the balls he caught, go over his treasured autographed paraphernalia, and plan the next trip to the ballpark.*

135

TARGET FRISBEE

Set a course of seven objects at which players will take turns throwing a Frisbee—a tree, a bush, a pole stuck in the ground. Players must track how many throws it took to hit their mark. The player with the lowest par for the course is the winner.

★ *Have red-and-white-striped bags filled with peanuts or popcorn to give out during the game.*

FAVORS

Sports trivia books in striped bags

Inexpensive hats

Sports stickers

Key chains with balls on them

MENU

CARAMEL CORN

HOT DOGS ON A STICK

MICROWAVE CORN ON THE COB

AUTOGRAPH CAKE

BOXED OR CANNED DRINKS

SHAKE, RATTLE, AND ROLL

TURNING UNEXPECTED EVENTS (from a broken water pipe to a blackout) into fun, or at least making the best of them, calls for some creative thinking and lots of good nature. But it can be done. Think of celebrating your "close call" (fire, storm, earthquake) in a block party. Invite the neighbors and recount your adventures. One family in a San Francisco neighborhood that got "all shook up" in the 1989 earthquake has done just that. October 17 (not yet an official national Earthquake Day) has become their day to relive the 1989 disaster and recount their blessings. Beverly Riehm has been the organizer, and her recipe for their party can be easily adapted for your own.

INVITATION

Invite all the families in the neighborhood by sending or delivering an invitation appropriate to the event you are commemorating. For their party marking the anniversary of the California earthquake, the Riehms sent out a piece of seismograph paper with the time and place of the party. Buy graph paper and draw an unbroken line of squiggles across the page. This is the only graphic needed. Write down the party details underneath the graph. Request that your guests bring a photograph album from that time.

For a broken water main, send out a photo or drawing of a fire hydrant. For a blackout or a hurricane, send out a small candle taped to your invitation.

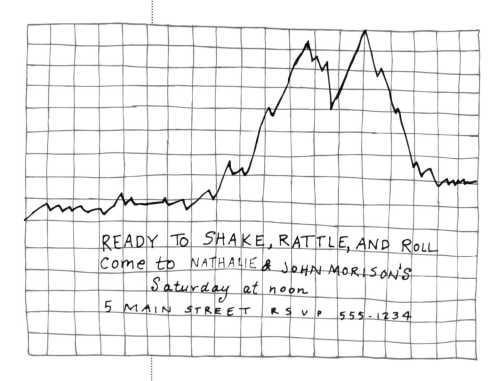

READY TO SHAKE, RATTLE, AND ROLL
Come to NATHALIE & JOHN MORISON'S
Saturday at noon
5 MAIN STREET   R S V P   555-1234

DECORATIONS

The only way to entertain a block party is outdoors, on the block, or in the yard. Cordon off the area by using black and yellow striped tape (or choose a portion of the back yard to string some of this tape). Buy or make yellow "Caution" signs to post around the yard. Use green, yellow, and red signs representing the signs posted by the police department after the quake. (The buildings were marked with these colors to designate their conditions: red meant "get out," yellow "use caution," and green meant "safe.") Set up flares in strategic places. Display quake photos by placing them on a table or tacking them on bushes or trees around the house.

ACTIVITIES

TOP TEN LISTS

Divide the guests into teams. Be sure to mix up the ages so that each team has both kids and adults on it. Ask the players in each group to list their top ten reasons for continuing to live in the area.

BEST PHOTO CAPTION AWARD

Select several of the quake pictures you have displayed in the yard for this activity. Have pads of paper and pencils handy for anyone who wants to enter the photo caption contest. Award prizes for the best quips.

★ *Atlanta psychologist Dr. Leslie Ward says, "Children need the opportunities for bringing back images and feelings after traumatic events. Telling stories and recollecting past events with people who have had like experiences are important to the healing process."*

SING FOR YOUR SUPPER

Require all the guests to sing a line from a song that had "shake" or similar words within the lyrics (e.g., "Shake, Rattle and Roll," "Twist and Shout," etc.) before they help themselves to the buffet line.

SAFETY TIPS

Especially if there are many children in the gathering, invite an official or have one of the grown-ups act the part and talk about safety precautions. List some do's and don'ts, and distribute the party favor bag afterward.

RELAYQUAKE

At the Levines' half-year party (a half year after the birthday of the twins, Cara and Jake, and the Los Angeles earthquake), their mom and dad arranged a sports extravaganza to let out some energy and show some humor about life. This relay race was the day's favorite.

Have as many fresh eggs as there are players. Place small step stools at various points in the back yard, each about 10 yards apart from the others. Station an "earthquake monitor" at each. On top of the first one, place an empty plastic container; at the second, a full cup of water and a plastic pitcher full of water; and at the third, a spray can of whipping cream.

Divide the guests into two teams. To begin, each player holds an egg in a soup spoon and runs with it to the first station. He places the egg in the plastic container and runs to the second station. There he drinks the cup of water, being careful not to spill any. When done, he runs to the third station, where the monitor sprays his mouth full of whipped cream. The player then returns to the starting point, where he touches the arm of the next player on his team, who starts again with his own egg. The winning team is the one that breaks no eggs, spills no water, and avoids getting whipped cream on the players' faces.

★ *Frank and Coleen Quinn, in Newport, Rhode Island, took a videotape of Hurricane Bob as he was "visiting." The next year, the Quinns' kids, Joey and Mary Catherine (ten and seven), invited all the neighborhood kids to come watch the video and relive the exciting experience together.*

FAVORS

Put together small survival kits for favors to take home. Include a small flashlight, bottled water, granola bars, batteries, pocketknife, and an emergency blanket in a bag.

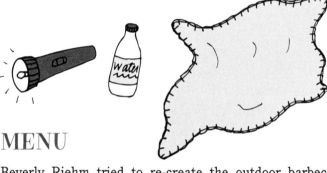

MENU

Beverly Riehm tried to re-create the outdoor barbecue food that her family and friends fixed out of necessity right after the quake. You can organize a potluck, or make everything yourself. Whatever the menu, try to find appropriate names for the offerings.

SHAKE-AND-QUAKE CHICKEN

JELLO JIGGLES

FAULTY FRIES

SEISMIC SALAD

BUMP-ALONG BROWNIES

SIMPLY SUMMER

SUMMER HOLIDAYS PRESENT THE BEST OPPORTUNITIES for spontaneous party giving. Kids, unencumbered by school and homework, have time to fill and excess energy to use. So choose a date and get everybody involved in planning and preparing. The party itself occurs for a couple of hours on a single day. The fun of the party starts much earlier and lasts far longer.

INVITATION

Make a fan out of colored paper (try one that is glossy on one side). Write or stencil these words: "Come cool off in the Smith's back yard (time, place, date, RSVP). Kids, bring your bikes."

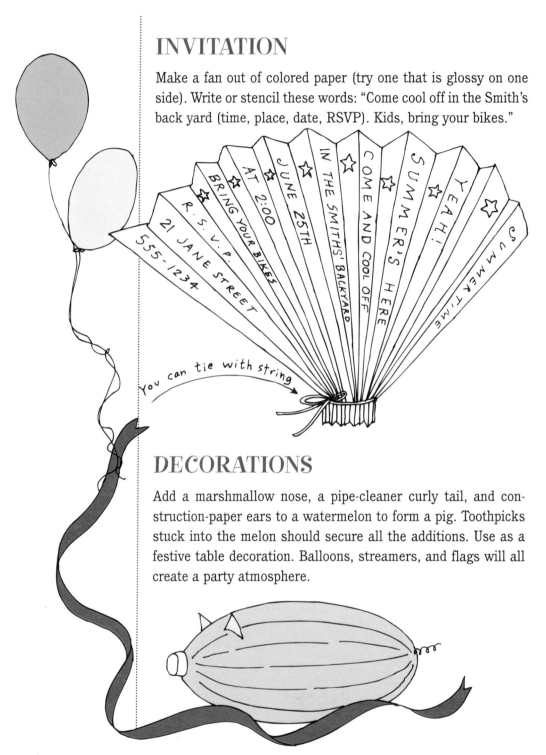

You can tie with string

DECORATIONS

Add a marshmallow nose, a pipe-cleaner curly tail, and construction-paper ears to a watermelon to form a pig. Toothpicks stuck into the melon should secure all the additions. Use as a festive table decoration. Balloons, streamers, and flags will all create a party atmosphere.

ACTIVITIES

BIKE DECORATING AND PARADE

Use the yard or garage as a work area. Assign each bike and owner a "parking spot" on arrival. Put out bike decorations in buckets and boxes so the bikers can start decorating as they arrive. Include rolls of crepe paper in different colors, tissue paper, ribbons, glue, several pairs of scissors, twist ties, clothespins, playing cards, plastic toys and charms, tin cans, strips of Mylar, bottle caps, and other decorating accessories. Award prizes for different categories of "best bikes" (the most unusual, most beautiful, most colorful, best use of a certain color, best theme, most outrageous, funniest, bike most like its owner, etc.).

Now prepare for the parade. Ride the bikes slowly around the neighborhood. Encourage neighbors to come out and view the parade. Take lots of pictures. Make a videotape of the parade to play back later to the riders and other guests.

★ *For some serious summer fun, fill a child's plastic swimming pool with water and dirt from the back yard to make the ultimate mud pies. Children and adults alike will want to get their hands (and maybe more) dirty.*

THREE-LEGGED RACE

Divide the guests into teams of two. Standing next to each other, the players in each pair tie their adjacent legs together. At the sound of the whistle, the unit must move toward the finish line as fast as possible. Whoever gets there first wins.

★ *Perry Heard and her two daughters, Lindsay and Erica, are always quick to take advantage of warm and sunny days in Maine. When it's picnic time, a few phone calls to invite friends and a combined effort in packing a lunch are all that's required to organize a picnic at the beach.*

BALLOON VOLLEYBALL

Set up a homemade volleyball net, tying a piece of rope between two chairs approximately 10 to 12 feet apart. Blow up a balloon that you will use as your ball. The teams take their positions on either side of the net. One side goes first, serving to the other team. The teams take turns hitting the balloon back and forth until one team misses, which gives the other team a point. Play until one team reaches a predetermined score.

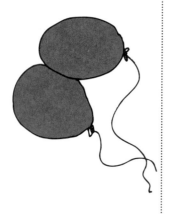

SUMMER CHALLENGE

Set up a challenge course in your backyard or park for guests to maneuver with their bikes (even young kids can do this using tricycles). This obstacle course is flexible, so you can add any other ideas you have for your summer fun.

★ *Find an adult who will happily impersonate Abraham Lincoln or Uncle Sam for the day. Invite him to join your July 4th celebration picnic by dressing up and delivering a patriotic address. Read the real thing—the Gettysburg Address or the Preamble to the Constitution or John F. Kennedy's Inaugural Address—or write your own version for added fun.*

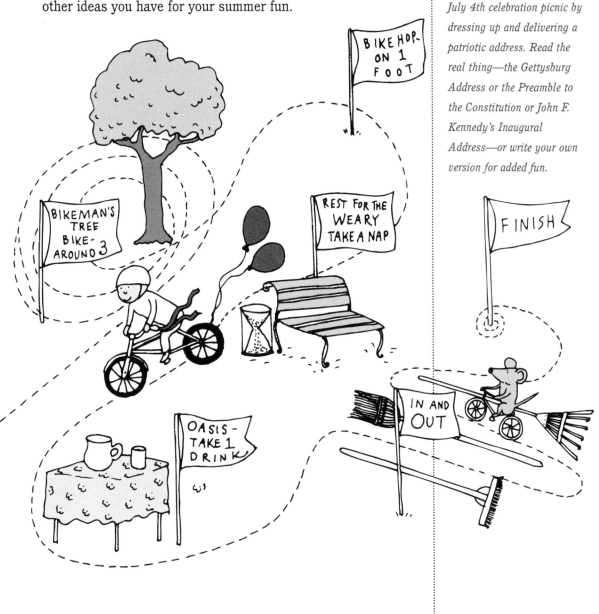

147

ELBOW TAG

Divide the players into pairs and have them link arms. The pairs join to make a large circle with at least 15 feet between them. Pick a pair and divide them—one player is "It" and the other is being pursued. If the player who is "It" can tag the other, he becomes "It." If the other player latches onto another couple and links elbows, she's safe. But the player she did not link elbows with must run and be chased until he is caught by "It" or hooks on with another couple.

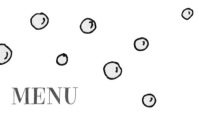

MENU

GRILLED SUMMER SPARE RIBS
WITH BARBECUE SAUCE

CORN ON THE GRILL

SUMMER GREEN SALAD

BAKED BEANS

CLASSIC BROWNIES

★ *If your children love playing with bubbles, see page 58 of the* Penny Whistle Party Planner *for some wonderful bubble ideas.*

SPRING FLING

SPRING FEVER GIVES YOU THE EXCUSE to give a wonderful party where the air is warm and breezy and everyone wants to dance and sing to celebrate the grateful arrival of sunshine and flowers. Revive an ancient custom and invite your friends and family to celebrate around the maypole.

★ *Diane Koge-Anders's twin boys loved the party where Mom made "mud" for the dessert. To make mud: crush Oreos, add chocolate pudding and chocolate cake mushed together (no exact measurements are needed), and scoop helpings into either plastic or clay pots. Add a plastic flower and/or gummy worms sticking out. The kids loved it!*

★ *You can line the clay pots with plastic wrap. to keep the food from having direct contact with the clay.*

INVITATION

Mini-umbrellas attached to a doily with party information on it.

DECORATIONS

For the indoor part of the party: Gather some old umbrellas and decorate them with glued-on buttons and beads. Tie lots of ribbons in different colors hanging from the spokes. Collect paper cutouts from magazines and glue those on. (You can also do this with your guests as an activity, and then display the finished umbrellas.)

ACTIVITIES

MAYPOLE

The maypole dance is a revival of an ancient fertility rite. In its oldest form, it was a circle dance around a tree. In the early 1900s, the tree was replaced by a decorated pole, which had become the symbol of spring. The dance itself can be quite simple—each participant holds the end of a 12-foot ribbon in his or her hand, and all participants simply weave the ribbon over and under around the maypole.

Maypole:

Use a flagpole at the park; a good size is 9 to 13 feet tall (that's the standard height of a maypole). Attach pairs of ribbons at the top of the pole. Ribbons should be approximately 3 feet longer than the pole, each with a loop at the end for a hand to slip through. Longer ribbons allow for more freedom of movement. Dancers "weave" their ribbons over and under each other to their favorite tune. When the dance is finished, secure the ribbons to the ground with clothespins.

CARNATION FANTASY

Start this project before your guests come. All you need is a bunch of white carnations, inexpensive glasses to use as vases, and some food coloring. Trim the ends of the carnations at an angle, and place each flower in an individual glass containing 2 inches of water and a few teaspoons of food coloring. Within twenty-four hours, the petals will have "magically" started to turn the color of the water, and they will continue to bloom over the next few days. Your guests can take the carnations home and continue to see the colors change.

★ *Put out colored pieces of yarn, old ribbon, and so on in a basket or pie tin for the birds and squirrels to use to make their nests. Take a walk around the neighborhood and search for your colors!*

PAPER GARLANDS

All you need is colored tissue paper, scissors, needle and thread, and small beads. Cut the tissue paper into 8" squares. Keep folding each individual piece into smaller squares, ending with a 1-inch square. Snip all off all 4 corners, creating an octagon. With needle and thread, go through the center of a tissue paper flower followed by a bead, followed by another tissue paper flower etc. Separate paper to resemble petals.

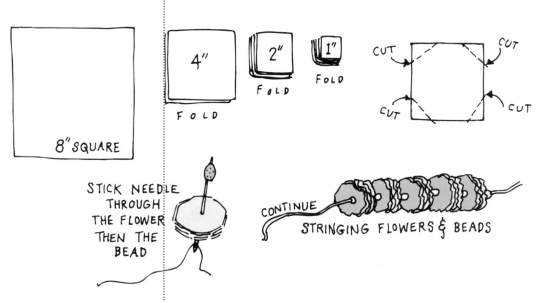

UMBRELLA MADNESS

Each guest should have an inexpensive umbrella from your local discount store. They can decorate them with ribbons, buttons, beads, tulle, silk flowers, and puff paints to make their own take-home treat for May showers. The more tulle and ribbons—especially in bright colors hanging from the spokes—the better!

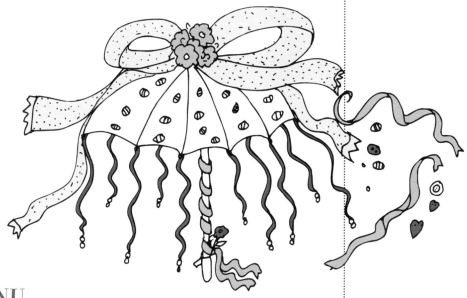

MENU

TEA

ASSORTED COOKIES

TRIFLE

FLOWERPOTS

MAY PARFAITS

LEMON FIZZY

STAMPEDE

CORRAL "THE WILD BUNCH" ON A DAY when there's too much pent-up energy and no school schedule in sight. Invite a few friends for an impromptu stampede party. Your call should indicate the time you're starting and ending (two hours is plenty), the party location (your back yard, a park, or—in a pinch—your family room), and a request to dress "Western."

Buy Western bandannas in two or three different colors. Arriving guests can choose a bandanna to wear throughout the party. The bandannas will make everyone a Westerner whether they're wearing full cowboy regalia or not. They will also serve as a convenient way of separating players into teams for the "cattle roundup relay."

INVITATION

Buy one bandanna for each invitation. Copy the cowboy boot below, and write the invitation copy on the boot, as we did. Fold the bandanna as if you were wearing it, and attach the boot to one end with string. Mail in a padded envelope.

★ *When Jon and Steve Root were eight and ten, they went camping in Yosemite, California. They were certain that there would be no food for them to eat and they would starve to death. So they brought with them every junk food you can imagine, and a five-pound newly opened can of peanut butter. When they woke up in the morning and looked outside, their food was strewn every-where—not eaten, just thrown all over the campsite.*

Camp rangers later confirmed that a bear had visited their campsite while they slept!

DECORATIONS: Western Motif

A piñata will serve as decoration and will add flavor to the party. It will make a fun activity when the guests take turns striking the piñata, breaking it open, and sharing its contents—candy. Hang it from a tree branch. You can make your own piñata (see page 66), or you can get one in a party-supply store, where piñatas of all different shapes and sizes are found. Look for a cowboy, a horse, a cowboy hat, or a cow to carry out the theme (or decorate them yourself).

Take instant photos of everyone and put them in "Wanted Poster" frames (use inexpensive mat board for frames and write WANTED on them with a marking pen). Use them to identify people by pinning them to the guests' clothes, or tack them to tree trunks.

ACTIVITIES

If your party is in the evening, play flashlight tag. Otherwise, try "The Sheriff."

FLASHLIGHT TAG

After dark, gather the guests and get out your flashlight. One player is "It" and holds the flashlight. At the signal, the other players chase "It." Whoever tags "It" first wins and is "It" for the next round.

THE SHERIFF SEZ

Start this game by designating someone for the role of sheriff. The sheriff faces the other players and gives commands that must be followed by the group as long as the command is preceded by the words "The Sheriff Sez." If an order is given without these words, such as "turn around" or "touch your toes," the player who forgets and obeys the order is out. Play until there is only one remaining.

LASSO THE BULL

Set up a bicycle draped with a blanket, leaving the handlebars free to act as the "horns." Tie 3-foot-long lengths of rope into nooses. Have players take turns trying to lasso the horns of the bicycle bull. Players score one point for each ring made. Whoever scores the most points after three rounds wins.

★ *Nancy Inglis and her family play a version of "The Sheriff Sez" called "Dracula, May I?" Dracula commands the other players to do the Zombie Zoom, the Vampire Vroom, or the Frankenstein Shuffle by saying, "You may . . . " The players have to copy the steps Dracula has demonstrated. If Dracula doesn't say "you may . . ." and the player complies, he has to return to the starting line.*

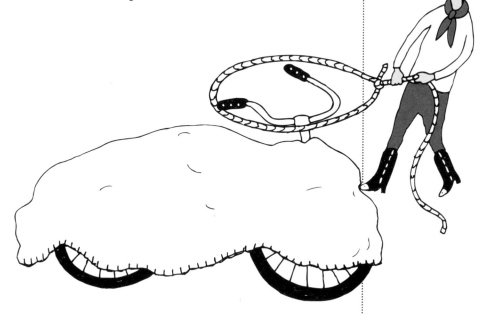

157

CATTLE ROUNDUP

Set up an obstacle course using markers of your choice. (You can use garbage cans, bean bags, briefcases, stuffed animals, etc.) Divide guests into two or three teams, and line up each team behind a starting line. Give the first member of each team a broom, and place a balloon or small ball at his feet. At the start, the first person of the first team follows the course, controlling the balloon with the broom, returning to the starting line, and passing the broom and ball to the second person, who goes next. After the first team has finished, the second team completes the relay, and then the third. A timer keeps track of the total amount of time it took each team to compete. The team with the fastest time wins. Give awards for first, second, and third place.

BUILD A TEPEE

One large tepee will be a haven for the kids to play in, whether it is in the back yard or the park grounds. The fun is to make this together with the kids so they see how a tepee is designed and will get a charge out of being able to construct it by hand. You will need eight 6-foot bamboo poles (available at lumber supply and garden supply stores), two dropcloths (available at paint supply stores), rope, masking tape, and large felt-tipped marking pens with wide tips. To begin, arrange the poles side by side on the ground. Tie the ends together about a foot from the top of the poles. Stand the whole pile of poles on the ground and spread the "legs" (the parts of the poles not tied together). You can push the spread ends of the poles into the ground so the tepee will be pretty stable. Drape the dropcloths over the poles, leaving an opening for a door. Tape them at various points to the poles so the cloth won't slide off. Now you can have the kids write and decorate all over the dropcloth with their large markers.

The kids are now ready to play in the tepee. Some kids, as Marc did when he and his friends built theirs, like to cover the ground so they complete their new "house." Marc brought out a small carpet that he had in his room. His friend Aaron Greenberg brought an old bathroom rug from his garage.

CAMPFIRE SING-ALONG

Join in round after round of everyone's favorites. If your location allows, build a campfire as the center for the sing-along.

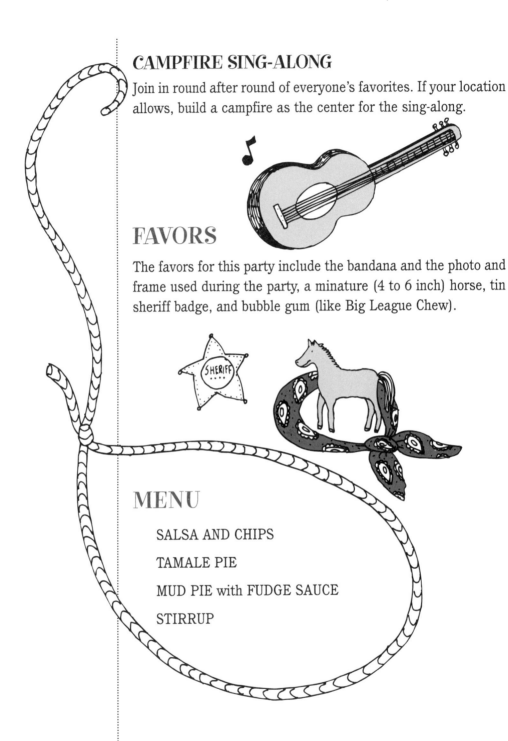

FAVORS

The favors for this party include the bandana and the photo and frame used during the party, a minature (4 to 6 inch) horse, tin sheriff badge, and bubble gum (like Big League Chew).

MENU

SALSA AND CHIPS

TAMALE PIE

MUD PIE with FUDGE SAUCE

STIRRUP

TIME-TRAVELING BIRTHDAY

TRAVELING THROUGH TIME IS EVERY CHILD'S DREAM—and the notion of this fantastic journey is a great idea for a birthday party. (We couldn't have a book concluding that any day is a holiday without mentioning at least one birthday party idea, now could we?) There are over fifty birthday parties in *The Penny Whistle Party Planner* and *The Penny Whistle Birthday Party Book*. You can celebrate this party on a birthday, for New Year's, or as an anniversary of any occasion, since you are celebrating the passage of time.

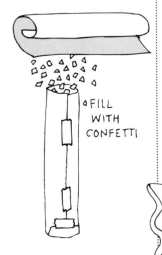

◁ FILL
WITH
CONFETTI

INVITATION

Make a Roman candle. Use one sheet of construction paper, confetti, colored paper, and tape. Roll the construction paper into a tube approximately 1 inch in diameter and 9 inches long. Tape the long edge of paper to the tube. Fold the tube in at one end. Load the candle loosely with the confetti. Tie the other end with a ribbon so the confetti won't fall out. Write information on the outside of the candle.

you are invited to ☆ ☆
ADAM JAEGER'S
TIME-TRAVELING PARTY
October 7th at NOON   555-1234

★ *Balloons can be decorated as clocks, and paper plates can be made into clocks and hung all over the house. Bring any clocks you have into the party area.*

DECORATIONS

Make more Roman candles to use as place cards. Hang streamers everywhere—some strung, others rolled so guests can throw them in celebration. Have horns and balloons in profusion. Use a white paper tablecloth. If your table is round, draw a table-size clock face; if it is rectangular, draw a grandfather clock. Use many clocks as centerpieces.

ACTIVITIES

MAKING HATS

Assemble tape, staplers, glue, puff paints, markers, glitter, glue, artificial flowers, ribbon, streamers, construction paper, feathers, and pompons so each guest can make and decorate his own hat. Use inexpensive felt hats, baseball caps, or painter's caps.

★ *You can make a time line on a large roll of paper listing all the pertinent events in the child's life (use fax or shelf paper rolls).*

WHO AM I?

Each player writes down the names of five historical figures on individual pieces of paper, folds them up, and puts them in the pot. Players are divided into teams of two. The first team starts by having one player pick a piece of paper from the hat and attempt to describe to his teammate qualities that will help him guess who the historical figure is. If the teammate answers correctly, they keep the slip, pick another, and continue until time runs out. If they can't get it or if time runs out before the teammate guesses correctly, the slip is returned to the pot. Each team takes a turn and then players change roles: he who asked questions tries to answer, and vice versa until all clues have been answered. Whoever collects the most clues wins.

UP WITH THE TIMES

Each guest is given a sheet of paper marked into seven divisions to resemble a diary. Each signs his name at the top, folds over the paper, and passes it to the player to his right. In not more than seven words, players write in Monday's space an account of what they did on that day. Then the diaries are passed to the right again after being carefully folded. The next player writes in the space for Tuesday. This continues until a full week has been entered. Then each in turn announces the name at the top of the page he's holding and reads the "confession."

RIDDLES

Write your answers down on a piece of paper:

★ What makes a striking gift?—*A clock.*

★ When is a clock dangerous?—*When it strikes one.*

★ What is time?—*Money.*

★ What is time and a fruit?—*A date.*

★ What is that which you have seen but will never see again?—*Yesterday.*

★ What comes once in a minute, twice in a moment, but not once in a thousand years?—*The letter M.*

★ What day of the year commands you to go forward?—*March 4th.*

164

BEAT THE CLOCK

You will need two boxes filled with old clothes and accessories (hats, shoes, bracelets, boas, scarves). Divide the guests into two teams. The object is for each player to run across the room, put on everything in the box, run back to his team, and take everything off. The next player has to put all the clothes on his body, run to the box, remove the clothes, and run back. The third player runs to the box, puts on the clothing, and so on. The first team to finish is the winner.

★ *Jill made a birthday chair for one of Remy's parties. It was painted in bright colors and every guest signed it on his or her way into the party. Many years later, Remy still has the chair.*

★ *Another version: Take all the cards (doubles of each) and mix. Turn all over, upside down, on a table or floor. Each player gets to turn over two cards at a time. One goal is to match two. When you don't, turn them over again in the same spot. Each player gets to turn over two at a time—when he gets a match, he goes again. The player with the most matches—sets of matching photos—wins.*

TIME TRAVELER LOTTO

Many lotto games are available in stores. But ever since Gary Gilbar made his own lotto game for Lisa and Marc out of photos of different things the family noticed on their trip to Paris, the Gilbars have enjoyed making their own lotto games. Here's how to make yours:

A lotto game is made up of picture cards and matching boards, each with six to nine pictures that match the picture cards. A couple of weeks before the party, take the camera, and together with the kids, take pictures of things you associate with time and travel. Clocks, maps, numbers, cars, airplanes, street signs—you get the idea. Develop the film, asking for an extra set of photos so you will have two of each picture you took, in the smallest size available.

Cut out pieces of cardboard 8 inches square. With a marker, divide equally into nine boxes. Paste a different photo on each square. Make a matching card with that photo on it. Make as many lotto boards as there will be players, and as many different cards as there are pictures.

To play, each player gets his own board. The cards are stacked, and each player gets to turn one card over at a time. The player who has the picture that is on the card on his board gets that card and places it on the matching picture on his board. The player whose board is covered first (just as in bingo) wins.

FAVORS

Plastic stopwatches or watches

Diaries

MENU

PIZZA CLOCKS

SALAD BAR

SUNDAE BAR

FORTUNE CUPCAKES

★ *Buy the game Beat the Clock for a fun time-filler to play as guests arrive.*

UNDER THE HARVEST MOON

FROM ONE END OF OUR EARTH TO THE OTHER, people find ways to celebrate a bountiful harvest at the end of a growing season. In the spirit of this tradition, pick a day—any day—and hold a harvest holiday. You can, of course, hold off until the traditional Thanksgiving Day or choose your own time to make some cranberry sauce. Whenever you honor the harvest, have a field day!

INVITATION

Smooth-skinned gourds can be found in great abundance during the fall. Pick out interesting shapes that are large enough to hold all the party invitation information (but make sure they are small enough to fit into a padded mailing envelope). Permanent wide-tipped marking pens will work best.

"There's a harvest moon, over the Larsens', Saturday, October 12, Come Shine with Us. RSVP."

THERE'S
A HARVEST MOON
OVER THE LARSENS'
SATURDAY ☆
OCTOBER 12
COME SHINE
WITH US
☆
R.S.V.P 555-1234

★ *Our friend Jane Paley made a scarecrow to place at her front door and dressed her as an old lady, which was disconcerting to her guests (not to mention the crows flying by).*

DECORATIONS

Wrap cardboard tubes in brown paper and stuff them with candy corn. Tubes should be approximately 6 inches long; wrapping paper should be 12 inches wide so that each end has a surplus 3 inches. Tie the ends with raffia ribbon. Write the names of your guests on each, and use as place cards. At the end of the party, these can be taken home as favors. Use gourds, fall leaves, branches with berries, and ears of dry corn for house decorations. Thanksgiving art projects from school can be displayed around the house. Pine-cone turkeys add to the atmosphere, and making them is the Wylers' family treat.

You'll need large pine cones, construction paper, scissors, glue, and some felt-tipped pens. First cut a turkey head from red construction paper and a beak from yellow construction paper (see drawings). Glue the beak to the head. Using markers, draw two eyes. Cut a half circle approximately 8 inches in diameter from colored construction paper—this will be the turkey's tail feathers. Cut triangles from the outer edge of the circle. Use a marker to draw texture on the feathers. Cut two feet from brown construction paper and glue to the body. Glue the head to the front of the pine cone and the feathers to the back. Use the turkey(s) as a centerpiece for the table, or find other areas around the house to display them.

170

Scarecrows also make unusual house props. They are traditionally used on farmland or in gardens to discourage birds from eating the crops. The scarecrow you make will probably not get that kind of work, but then the scarecrow in *The Wizard of Oz* wasn't doing his ordinary thing, either!

Scarecrows can be made entirely from hay or straw or with other materials. Why don't you find a few places to add straw for the right effect (peeking out from under a hat or out of a sleeve, for instance). Since they do resemble the human form, they almost become additional guests and are certain to be conversation provokers!

To make your scarecrow, construct the figure by stuffing an old pair of jeans and flannel shirt with rags or crumpled-up newspaper. A ball or an inflated balloon will make a head. Forget facial features—just add a big, slouchy hat that covers most of the head. Tufts of straw should emerge from under the hat. Prop the scarecrow against a chair or in a corner. Tack him to a wall, if necessary.

★ *Jill Weber made a scarecrow for Remy's twelfth birthday. He had a pumpkin head, a cowboy hat, potato ears, and a carrot nose stuck in with toothpicks. He was placed outside the door, with one arm pointing toward the door and the other with a bottle of beer. He also had a pipe dangling from his mouth.*

ACTIVITIES

THE "HA" GAME

The object of this game is to remain straight-faced, which is quite difficult under the circumstances. Players are not allowed to laugh. They lie on the floor with their heads on each other's stomachs. The first player says, "Ha." The second, "Ha, ha." Each player adds another "ha" at his turn. Continue playing the game until someone can't help but laugh. Laughers are eliminated until only one or two remain. Have prizes ready for the winners.

THE TURKEY GAME

The contestants in this pencil-and-paper game all try to be the first to complete a drawing of a turkey. All you need is a pencil and paper for each player and one pair of dice. Each guest takes a turn rolling the dice, attempting to get a pair of sixes so that he may start drawing his picture of a turkey. Then a player will need the following numbers to complete the drawing; the first to finish is the winner:

2 sixes: BODY

a number 2: LEG

a number 3: TOE

a number 4: NECK

a number 5: WATTLE

a number 6: EYEs

adding to 7, 8, 9, 10, 11: FIVE TAIL FEATHERS

THE PIG CARD

Deal a deck of cards between players. In the middle of the table, place a pile of clothespins (or any other accessory that can be counted in multiples), one less in number than the group of players. To start, each player passes one card, face down, to the person on the right. Each player, trying to get four cards of a kind, continues passing only those he does not want. When he does get four of a kind, he quietly places them face down on the table and, as inconspicuously as possible, reaches over and picks up a clothespin. Of course, the minute anyone notices this, they follow suit. Soon everyone is grabbing for a clothespin, and since there's one short, someone is left without one, thereby earning a P—the first letter in PIG. Rounds continue until someone becomes the PIG and loses. Everyone continues to play until there is only one player left.

TURKEY WALK RELAY RACE

Divide your guests into two teams. As someone says "GO," the first person on each team starts out crossing the left foot behind right, the right foot behind the left, and so on, trying to progress, like a turkey, about 4 inches forward on each step. The players continue walking like this until they reach the goal line, come back, and touching the next person in line, who does the same thing. The first team to complete the relay wins.

FEATHER RELAY

Moving a feather from one side of a room to the other is a difficult task. Challenge your guests with this game. First, divide the guests into two teams. Place two strings on the floor about twelve paces from each other. Divide each team in half. Have half of one team stand behind one string and the other half of the team stand behind the other string. Do the same for the second team.

At the sound of the whistle, the first player from each team starts blowing a feather across the room to his team member. If the feather falls to the floor, the player must pick it up and keep going. The team member must then blow the feather back across the room to another teammate. Each member will have a turn. The first team to complete the race is the winner. *Note:* If the players are preschoolers, they will have an easier time tapping a balloon than blowing a feather.

MENU

Eat dinner by candlelight.

CORN SOUP

MULLED CIDER

OLD-FASHIONED CHICKEN POT PIE

CORNBREAD MUFFINS

PUMPKIN WITH BAKED APPLES AND ICE CREAM

SALAD WITH VINAIGRETTE DRESSING

WELCOME HOME, BABY!

THE SIBLINGS OF A NEW BABY ARE UNDOUBTEDLY as excited as anyone else when the additional family member appears. Even though much fuss and attention is naturally focused on the baby's arrival, siblings will be happy to share the spotlight when they are included in the low-key festivities. When Annie brought Marc home from the hospital, she found that Lisa (who was then five years old) and Gary had decorated the house as a welcome for the new baby. There was a giant banner, which Lisa had drawn, balloons and streamers over the doorways, and a giant blowup of the birth announcement that Gary had designed. As Annie put Marc to bed in his new home, Grandmas Sylvia Gilbar and Essie Barbasch put together a homecoming dinner for the family to celebrate together. In fact, such an intimate party just for the family was truly what the doctor ordered.

Here are some ideas to help the whole clan get into the act.

★ *Our illustrator, Jill Weber, has developed her own image font called Baby Boom that includes babies and baby items as part of it's alphabet. It is available exclusively through FontHaus, Inc., 1-800-942-9110 for Macintosh computers.*

DECORATIONS

Make a "Welcome Home, Mom and (baby's name)" sign and hang it in a prominent place. Include some photos, if available. Any child-created banner, whether a "masterpiece" or not, should be treated as a work of art! Computer-generated designs or simply crepe-paper streamers and confetti (the New Year's celebrations variety) immediately give a room a party-like atmosphere. Hang pictures of the baby's siblings around the baby's new room.

Many new mothers get flowers in the hospital and at home. Annie's practice was adopted by many of her friends—pull a few stems out for individual vases in the older children's rooms so they feel a part of the celebration.

WELCOME HOME! MOM and CASSIE

ACTIVITIES

Any activities at this time should not put any extra pressure on the new mom. However, siblings do want to feel included in the family, so these projects are for kids to do, sometimes with the help of other adults. Begin by taking pictures of the new baby. Even little children can press the camera button. Don't put your prize camera at risk, but if there is an inexpensive one around the house (or if you like, you can buy a disposable camera) put it to use. Develop the photos ASAP so that the scrapbooks can be worked on immediately. Think about ordering duplicate photographs for grandparents and friends. Include captions that the kids write themselves.

★ A few weeks ahead of the expected delivery, it's important to prepare a questionnaire. Ask all the family members and close friends to answer the following:

1. What will the baby's name be?

2. How much will the baby weigh?

3. Is it a she or a he?

4. What's the exact date of the baby's arrival?

5. What is the time of arrival?

Put away the answers. When everyone gets home from the hospital, the "pool" should be brought out and a winner declared.

★ Include a sibling on a shopping trip for the new baby supplies. Even a small offering, such as a rattle or a pair of booties, when gift-wrapped and presented by the giver, can be a very meaningful experience.

★ *Don't forget the family dog. We know of one little Scottie named Piper whose nose was so out of joint when baby Andrea arrived that his first act was to "lift his leg" on the leg of the bassinet.*

★ *Ronna Gordon, of Montecito, California, has given many baby showers, both larger for friends and small at home celebrations for her own babies. Her wonderful idea: She always serves baby fruits and vegetables to her guests. These are available in many large markets and look wonderful arranged on platters.*

★ *When brand-new Christopher Hogan came home, flowers and all, his mom, Karen, presented a miniature cactus to older sister Michelle from her new little brother. She loved it.*

★ Choose some baby-related words, write them on a piece of paper, and scramble them up. Make copies for all the guests. Allow everyone a set time to solve the "All Mixed Up" word game.

Some examples:

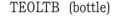
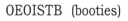

TEOLTB (bottle)

OEOISTB (booties)

PEDIRA (diaper)

BBYA (baby)

RABE (bear)

LOLD (doll)

SYTO (toys)

RBCI (crib)

★ Children in every family seem to have their own board game favorites—Scrabble, Pictionary, Monopoly, Chutes and Ladders, Checkers, etc. This is an excellent time to play them together.

★ Finally, as a surprise, have some party favors ready for the older siblings. They don't have to be elaborate; it's the thought that matters. Paper party bags filled with balloons, felt-tipped markers, and some miniature toys all wrapped as gifts will be great hits. Get some disposable cameras and hand one to each child. Each child can then be in charge of taking a whole roll of pictures himself.

BREAKFAST, LUNCH, AND DINNER
(one or all prepared by the kids)

Adult help is required, but it is amazing what kids can do by themselves. Their accomplishments should never be underestimated. Start with the premise that this is their party, and consequently they determine what food will be served, the look of the table, and the dress for the occasion.

First, the atmosphere will feel more like a party with some decorations. How about using some of the same props that are used for baby showers? Some of these parties use baby bottles without tops for drinks, cloth diapers for napkins, paper plates decorated with pictures of the baby's name. Teething rings become napkin holders, doll furniture is used for flower vases. And remember—photograph everything for the albums!

Balloons are always festive, and a few small "party favors" for everyone will balance the huge "attention on the newborn" factor.

MENU

Here are some suggestions for menu ideas that can be handled by kids (usually some adult help is essential). Use our ideas, or substitute your tried-and-true recipes as long as they are easy to do.

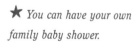

BREAKFAST	LUNCH	DINNER
MELON BALLS	PEANUT BUTTER AND BANANA SANDWICHES	TACOS
CINNAMON TOAST	STRAWBERRY FLIP	CHILLY CHOCOLATE PIE
	LEMONADE	

★ *Nadine Barbasch just couldn't wait until her sister Emily arrived. She planned all kinds of games and presents for the new baby. Her mom, Lynne, encouraged Nadine to make many lists and plans, knowing that her excitement will go a long way to making her especially happy and prepared when Emily finally arrived. And it worked—Emily's arrival was greeted with much fanfare and love, with Nadine leading the celebration.*

★ *You can have your own family baby shower.*

RECIPES

LIQUID AND DRY MEASURE EQUIVALENCIES

Customary	Metric
¼ teaspoon	1.25 milliliters
½ teaspoon	2.5 milliliters
1 teaspoon	5 milliliters
1 tablespoon	15 milliliters
1 fluid ounce	30 milliliters
¼ cup	60 milliliters
⅓ cup	80 milliliters
½ cup	120 milliliters
1 cup	240 milliliters
1 pint (2 cups)	480 milliliters
1 quart (4 cups)	960 milliliters (.96 liters)
1 gallon (4 quarts)	3.84 liters
1 ounce (by weight)	28 grams
¼ pound (4 ounces)	114 grams
1 pound (16 ounces)	454 grams
2.2 pounds	1 kilogram (100 grams)

OVEN TEMPERATURE EQUIVALENCIES

Description	Degrees Fahrenheit	Degrees Celsius
Cool	200	90
Very slow	250	120
Slow	300–325	150–160
Moderately slow	325–350	160–180
Moderate	350–375	180–190
Moderately hot	375–400	190–200
Hot	400–450	200–230
Very Hot	450–500	230–260

BRACES OFF

MEAT LOAF BURGERS

2 pounds lean ground sirloin

4 tablespoons mayonnaise

4 eggs

½ cup minced green bell pepper

½ cup minced onion

16 large pimiento-stuffed green olives, chopped

2 cups shredded sharp cheddar cheese

2 large tomatoes, diced

1½ cups chopped white mushrooms

4 tablespoons wheat germ or bread crumbs

¼ teaspoon garlic powder

Salt and pepper to taste

Oil for frying

Combine the meat, mayonnaise, eggs, bell pepper, onion, olives, cheese, tomatoes, mushrooms, wheat germ, garlic powder, salt, and pepper. Mix together and form the mixture into eight patties, each about 1 inch thick. Sauté in a nonstick pan. Cook to the desired doneness. Serve on buns and garnish with tomatoes, sliced onions, slices of pickles, lettuce, etc.

SERVES 8.

CORN ON THE COB

Leave each corn cob intact. If you remove the husks, wrap the corn in a paper towel and place in the microwave oven for three minutes. Unwrap and remove the corn cob. Dab with melted butter and sprinkle lightly with salt. You should be able to cook about four ears of corn at a time.

CARAMEL APPLES

Caramel candies (one bag, 7 ounces of caramels, for every 8 apples)

1 wooden ice cream stick per apple

1 apple per guest, well washed

1 cupcake paper per apple

Melt the caramels in a pan over low heat, stirring often. Insert a stick into the base of each apple. Dip each apple into the melted caramel. Allow the caramel apples to cool on buttered wax paper. When cool and hardened, place the apples in individual cupcake holders.

CAMP RUNAMOK

CREAMY COLESLAW

Start this salad the day before and add the finishing touches before the party starts. Pack slaw in a covered plastic container and keep in a cooler.

1 small head cabbage
1 cup cider vinegar
1 tablespoon sugar
1 teaspoon salt
½ cup mayonnaise
½ cup sour cream
Salt and pepper to taste

Shred the cabbage into very, very thin slices. Place in a bowl with the vinegar, sugar, and salt; mix lightly. Let stand overnight in refrigerator. In the morning, drain off the vinegar (you can save to use in other salad dressings). Add the mayonnaise and sour cream to cabbage and mix lightly. Season with salt and pepper.

SERVES 8.

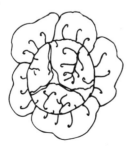

CAMP STEW

2 onions
8 carrots
2 tablespoons vegetable oil
2 pounds cubed beef
4 cups beef broth or water
Salt and freshly ground
*   black pepper*
2 cucumbers
⅓ cup fresh dill leaves
2 cups elbow macaroni or
*   tiny pasta such as orzo*

Finely chop the onion. Peel and slice the carrots ½ inch thick. Heat the oil in a large saucepan over medium heat. Add the onion and sauté, stirring frequently, until it is translucent—about 5 minutes. Add the beef, increase the heat to high, and sauté until the beef begins to brown—about 10 minutes. The beef will release lots of water, but don't be alarmed. Add the broth and bring it to a boil over medium heat. Cover and simmer gently for 10 minutes.

With a spoon, remove any scum that has risen to the surface. Add the carrots to the beef and season to taste with salt and pepper. Cover and simmer over low heat until the beef is tender, about 40 minutes more.

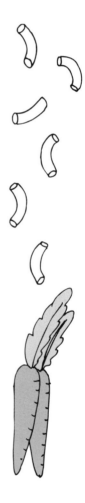

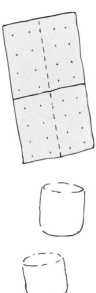

Meanwhile peel, seed, and cut the cucumber into ½-inch cubes. Mince the dill.

When the beef is done, stir in the pasta and simmer, covered, until tender, about 10 minutes more. Add the cucumber and dill and let the stew stand, off the heat and covered, for 10 minutes to warm the cucumber without cooking it through. Adjust the seasoning and serve hot in bowls.

SERVES 10.

S'MORES FOR ONE :

2 marshmallows
½ chocolate bar
2 graham crackers

Toast the two marshmallows on a toasting fork over the fire until they are golden brown. Place a piece of chocolate bar between two graham crackers. Slide the marshmallow from the toasting fork between the two graham crackers. Smoosh the whole thing together and eat.

MAKES 1 SERVING.

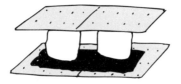

THE CASE OF THE MISSING TOOTH

CHEESE TORTILLAS

1 flour tortilla
1 slice thinly sliced ham
1 slice Monterey jack cheese
1 leaf lettuce
Honey mustard

Warm the tortilla and layer the rest of the ingredients on top. Roll up and secure with a toothpick.

SERVES 1.

BLUE CORN CHIPS

BABY TOOTH COOKIES

2 cups flour
2 teaspoons baking powder
½ cup butter
1 cup sugar
1 egg, beaten
¼ cup milk
¼ teaspoon vanilla

Sift the flour. Mix the baking powder with one cup of the flour and set aside. In the food processor, or by hand, cream the butter and the sugar. Add the egg, milk, and vanilla and keep creaming.

Gradually add the flour/baking powder mixture. Mix well. Add the remaining cup of the flour and mix again.

Gather the dough in a ball, cover with plastic wrap, and put into the refrigerator for about 2 hours.

Preheat the oven to 375 degrees. Flour a cutting board. Roll out half of the dough at a time to a sheet of dough about ¼ inch thick. Cut with a cookie cutter in different shapes. Sprinkle with cinnamon or sugar. Grease cookie sheets and place the cookies on them. Bake for 8 to 10 minutes.

HOMEMADE ICE CREAM
(see page 38)

DAY OF THE DRAGON

FORTUNE COOKIES
- *½ cup sugar*
- *2 egg whites, unbeaten*
- *Pinch of salt*
- *¼ cup butter or margarine, melted*
- *¼ cup flour*
- *¼ teaspoon vanilla extract*

Prepare 15 fortunes on 2½- by ½-inch slips of paper. Make them funny and/or sweet. Preheat the oven to 350 degrees. In a mixing bowl, stir the sugar into the egg whites. Add a pinch of salt. When the sugar is fully dissolved, add the butter, flour, and vanilla and beat with a mixer until smooth. Grease a cookie sheet. Drop the batter, one teaspoon at a time, 2 inches apart on the cookie sheet. Bake for 5 minutes, or until the edges are brown.

Remove the cookies from the oven and put them on a wooden cutting board. Put a fortune across the center of each circle of cookie and fold over to a semicircle. Lay the semicircle on the edge of a mixing bowl and bend it over the outside; hold it there for a few seconds until it holds shape. Keep working fast until all the cookies are made. MAKES ABOUT 15.

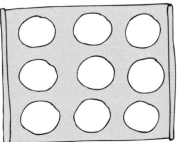

Here are some ideas for fortunes:

★ *Money will come your way*
★ *Study and you will receive A's*
★ *The boy/girl you like likes you, too*
★ *A new friend will soon be made*
★ *You will win your soccer game this weekend*
★ *Your teacher will forget to assign homework tomorrow*

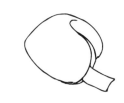

185

JENNY'S PEANUT BUTTER NOODLES

1 (8-ounce) package linguine

2 to 3 tablespoons creamy peanut butter

½ teaspoon salt

2 tablespoons soy sauce

1 tablespoon sesame oil

1 teaspoon sugar

½ teaspoon white wine vinegar

2 cloves garlic, crushed

1 teaspoon chopped onion

Cook the linguine according to package instructions. Drain. In a large mixing bowl, mix all of the remaining ingredients. Add the linguine to the sauce and coat well.

SERVES 8.

EARTH DAY

BARBECUED CHICKEN CHEESEBURGERS

3½ pounds ground chicken

1 cup chopped onions

1 teaspoon thyme

2 cups barbecue sauce

12 slices of American cheese

12 hamburger buns, toasted

12 slices tomato

Washed lettuce leaves

Mix the chicken, onions, and thyme in a bowl. (If you can, marinate in some of the barbecue sauce until you are ready to cook.) Make 12 balls with your hands. Flatten to about ½-inch-thick patties. Place on the barbecue. Baste often with the barbecue sauce. Cook until done. When done, place a slice of cheese on top of each patty and cook until it melts a little. Place the chicken burgers into the buns and garnish with the tomato slices and lettuce.

Have pickles, relish, mustard, and sliced onions ready for extra garnishes.

MAKES 12.

MAPLE LEAF SANDWICHES

Cream cheese

Jelly

2 slices wheat bread

Spread cream cheese and jelly on one slice of bread and top with the other slice. Look for leaf-shaped cookie cutters at cooking shops in your area; use them to cut the sandwiches, or use the template provided.

SWEET POTATO CHIPS

Heat 3 inches of vegetable oil in a wok to 375 degrees. Peel sweet potatoes and slice them with a slicer or in a food processor to the desired thickness. Fry until crisp. Drain on paper towels. Season with salt, or for a more interesting taste, season with superfine sugar and cinnamon. (You can also bake the chips in a 350-degree oven until crisp but not brown.)

CHOCOLATE CAKE

3 1-ounce squares
    unsweetened chocolate
⅔ cup sugar
½ cup milk
1 beaten egg
½ cup shortening
1 cup sugar
1 teaspoon vanilla
2 eggs
2 cups sifted cake flour
1 teaspoon soda
¼ teaspoon salt
⅔ cup milk

Preheat oven to 350 degrees.

Combine the chocolate, ⅔ cup sugar, ½ cup milk, and beaten egg in a saucepan.

Cook and stir over low heat until the chocolate melts and the mixture thickens; let it cool. Stir the shortening to soften. Gradually add 1 cup of sugar, creaming until light and fluffy. Add the vanilla. Add the 2 eggs, one at a time, beating well after each.

Sift together the flour, soda, and salt. Add to the creamed mixture alternately with ⅔ cup milk, beginning and ending with the flour mixture; beat after each addition. Blend in the chocolate mixture.

Bake in two paper-lined 9- x 1½-inch round pans for 25 to 30 minutes or until done. When the cake is done, stick lollipops into the top of the cake to make it look like a flower garden.

★ *You can make a tarantula cake. Use your favorite carrot cake recipe. Cover with cream cheese frosting. Use M&M's for the eyes and mouth. Decorate with black licorice for the legs.*

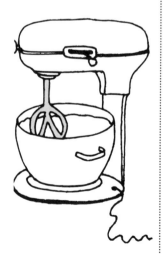

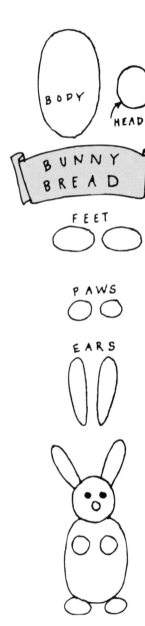

BODY

HEAD

BUNNY
BREAD

FEET

PAWS

EARS

EGGSTRAVA-GANZA

EGG NESTS

*2 (14.5-ounce) cans
    tomatoes*
¼ cup chopped onions
½ cup chopped green pepper
1 bay leaf
1 cup diced celery
Salt and pepper to taste
1½ cups soft bread crumbs
*2 cups shredded cheddar
    cheese*
8 eggs

Combine tomatoes, onions, green pepper, bay leaf, and diced celery in a saucepan on low heat on stove. Cook slowly until celery is tender. Remove bay leaf. Season to taste with salt and pepper. Add bread crumbs and pour half of the mixture into a greased 1½-quart casserole. Sprinkle with 1 cup cheddar cheese. Pour other half of mixture into casserole and sprinkle with remaining cheese. Make depression with tablespoon and break eggs into those depressions. Season to taste. Bake at 350 for 35 to 40 minutes.

SERVES 8.

BASKET OF MINIATURE VEGETABLES

BUNNY BREAD

*1 (1-pound) loaf frozen
    bread dough from 1
    (3-pound) package,
    thawed (see note below)*
1 large egg, lightly beaten
Assorted jelly beans
Ribbon

Note: To defrost the dough, thaw in the microwave oven. Place the dough in a microwave dish and cover with plastic wrap. Cook on the defrost cycle or low (10%) power for 6 to 8 minutes, rotating the dish occasionally; do not overthaw or the dough will begin to rise. The dough can also be thawed in its package overnight in the refrigerator.

Heat oven to 375 degrees. Grease a large cookie sheet. Cut thawed bread dough into 6 equal pieces. Shape 2 pieces into large flat ovals for bunny bodies; shape 2 pieces into round balls for bunny heads. Cut remaining 2 pieces into 6 pieces each, for a total of 12 pieces; shape 4 pieces into ovals for feet, 4 into balls for front paws, and the remaining into 4 into 2-inch-long ear shapes.

Place bodies on prepared cookie sheet well apart from each other. Attach heads, feet, paws, and ears to each body. Brush bunnies with beaten egg. Bake bread for 20 minutes until golden. Using wide spatula, carefully remove from cookie sheet and let cool completely on a wire rack.

Use jelly beans to decorate the bunnies while still warm. Press gently but firmly into surface. As the bread is still warm, the candies will adhere to its surface. If desired, tie a ribbon around the necks of the bunnies.

COOKIE BONNETS

Buy sugar cookies and dip into melted white chocolate, coating tops and sides. Place them on a wire rack to dry. For a thicker coat, redip after 5 minutes. Cut large marshmallows crosswise in half. Dip into the chocolate and center on cookie with cut side down. Decorate "brim" of hat with small flowered candies

and red-hot hearts. Chill 30 minutes before serving to set.

EASTER BASKET BREAD

Our friend Geri Jansen has been making this bread for the past four Easter celebrations with great success.

1 cup sugar

¾ stick butter or margarine

3 eggs

1 teaspoon almond flavoring

4–5 cups sifted flour

3 heaping teaspoons baking powder

½ cup orange juice (pulp juice is fine)

4 colored Easter eggs

1 egg yolk

confettini

Preheat the oven to 350 degrees. Combine the sugar, butter or margarine, eggs, and almond flavoring. In a separate bowl, combine the flour and baking powder. Mix together, adding the orange juice. You want the mixture to form one large ball. Keep adding additional flour as needed to get a good consistency. Make approximately 4 smaller balls (reserve a small amount to make the handles)

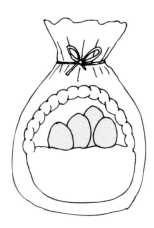

and press each onto a cookie sheet sprayed with cooking spray. Press the colored Easter eggs into the middle of the cakes. Roll out two pieces of the reserved mixture, approximately 2 to 3 inches each, and braid them. Place over the Easter eggs to make the "handle." Brush each cake with the egg yolk, sprinkle with confettini, and bake for 25 minutes. Be careful that the bottoms don't burn.

Wrap each basket in colored cellophane.

MAKES 4 BREADS.

FRIDAY THE 13TH

NIGHTCRAWLERS

12 large apples
1 (8-ounce) jar boysenberry jam
4 tablespoons butter
12 gummy worms

Preheat the oven to 350 degrees. Core the apples from the stem end to ½ inch from the bottom. Do not push through. Stuff each hole with 1 teaspoon each of jam and butter.

Place in a pan and bake uncovered for 35 to 45 minutes, depending on the size of the apples. When done, the apples should be tender but not mushy. Remove from the oven. Let cool.

Now set each apple in a bowl and spoon syrup from the baking pan around it. In the top of each apple, insert a gummy worm with at least half of its body protruding.

MAKES 12.

ABRACADABRA

1 whole-wheat tortilla
1 tablespoon peanut butter
2 tablespoons applesauce
1 tablespoon raisins
Dash of cinnamon

Warm the tortilla. Spread the remaining ingredients down the center of the tortilla. Roll up and serve.

MAKES 1.

LUCKY ROLL-UP

1 tortilla
1 slice Monterey jack cheese

Warm the tortilla and place one slice of cheese in center. Roll up and serve.

MAKES 1.

GHOULISH GUACAMOLE

4 ripe avocados, mashed

1 tomato, peeled and chopped

2 tablespoons finely chopped onions

2 tablespoons lemon juice

Salt and pepper to taste

Dash of Tabasco

Combine all the ingredients in the food processor and mix for 15 seconds. Return the avocado seeds to the mixture to keep it from turning brown. Store covered in the refrigerator until ready to serve. Serve with carrot and celery sticks and taco chips (try the black ones).

MAKES 3 CUPS.

SKELETON COOKIES

1 cup (2 sticks) butter

½ cup sugar

2 egg yolks

1 teaspoon almond or vanilla extract

2 cups flour

Preheat the oven to 350 degrees.

Mix all the ingredients together. Roll out ½ inch thick. Use a gingerbread boy cookie cutter to cut out cookies. Bake the cookies for about 12 minutes. Let cool. Ice with icing you've tinted with black food coloring and pipe on the skeletons' features with white icing (see drawing).

ICING

2 cups powdered sugar

3 tablespoons butter or margarine

Pinch of salt

1 tablespoon vanilla extract

2 tablespoons heavy cream

Sift the sugar. In a food processor fitted with the steel blade, blend the butter until smooth. Gradually add the sugar until creamy. Then add the salt and vanilla. Don't worry if the consistency is off; you can fix it by adding the cream. Color ¼ of the icing with black food coloring to use to accent the skeleton's features.

ICE WITH BLACK ICING

PIPE ON SKELETON WITH WHITE ICING

★ *You can also buy black icing at party supply stores*

GO FLY A KITE

KITE SANDWICHES

Dijon mustard
2 slices sourdough bread
1 slice turkey
1 slice Swiss cheese
Lettuce

Spread the mustard on one slice bread. Assemble turkey, cheese, and lettuce and top with other slice of bread. Cut sandwich into diamond shape and serve.

SERVES 1.

FRUIT KEBOBS

Make your own fruit kebobs. Cut up different types of fruit into cubes (melon, banana, apples, pears) and put them in individual bowls. Sprinkle with lemon juice to keep from turning brown. Add strawberries and grapes. Have two wooden skewers for each guest. Allow individuals to make their own kebobs to their taste. Figure four pieces of fruit per kebob.

CHOCOLATE DIP

½ cup half-and-half
*4 ounces bittersweet choco-
late, finely chopped*
*1 ounce milk chocolate,
finely chopped*
¼ teaspoon vanilla

In a small saucepan, bring the half-and-half to a simmer. Remove the pan from the heat. Stir in the chocolates until melted. Add the vanilla and stir until smooth. Pour the chocolate dip into a fondue pot over a Sterno flame. Arrange the fruit kebob buffet and allow guests to dip in turn, blow, and eat immediately.

SNAPPIN' SALAD

1½ cups snow peas
6 cups lettuce
2 tablespoons parsley
½ cup chopped fresh basil

Blanch snow peas in boiling water until bright green, about 1 minute. Drain and plunge peas into a bowl of ice water to stop cooking. Toss with vinaigrette.

VINAIGRETTE

3 tablespoons olive oil
1 tablespoon lemon juice
Pinch of salt and pepper

POTATO SALAD

2 pounds boiling potatoes (skin left on)

2 bunches green onions, chopped

½ cup flat-leaf parsley

Salt and pepper to taste

Lemon juice to taste

Dijon mustard, to taste

1 cucumber, peeled and thinly sliced

¾ cup mayonnaise

⅛ teaspoon paprika

2 garlic cloves, peeled and pressed

¼ cup virgin olive oil

Boil the potatoes until tender. Quarter, but do not peel. Combine remaining ingredients and mix well. Toss the potatoes with the dressing and serve.

GRADUATION

STAR PIZZAS (individual)

Baby Boboli (or other prepared pizza shell)

4 tablespoons seasoned tomato sauce

¼ cup grated mozzarella cheese

Preheat the oven to 450 degrees.

Cut the pizza shell into the shape of star. Spoon the tomato sauce onto the pizza shell and top with cheese. Heat the pizza until the cheese is melted and serve immediately.

FRUIT POPS

Bananas, large strawberries, pineapple circles, and several grapes on kebob sticks with tips broken off.

CLASS CUPCAKES

1 cup (2 sticks) butter or margarine, softened

2 cups sugar

3 eggs

3 cups all-purpose flour, sifted

½ teaspoon baking soda

½ teaspoon salt

1 cup plain yogurt

2 tablespoons fresh lemon or lime juice

Preheat the oven to 325 degrees.

Grease a 9-cup muffin pan (if you prefer, use paper liners). In a food processor fitted with the steel blade or with your electric mixer,

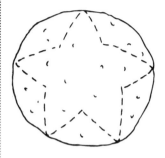

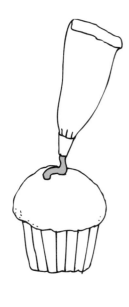

blend together the butter and sugar until they are soft and smooth. Add the eggs one at a time, blending after each addition. In another bowl, sift together the flour, baking soda, and salt. Mix into the butter mixture, alternating with the yogurt. Now add the lemon juice and mix in well. Pour the cupcake batter into the greased muffin pan, filling each cup ¾ full. Bake in the middle of the oven for 30 minutes. Test for doneness with a knife; if it comes out clean, the cupcakes are ready. Let cool for 15 to 30 minutes.

WHITE FROSTING

¾ cup sugar

½ teaspoon cream of tartar

2 egg whites

¼ cup cold water

2 teaspoons vanilla extract

In the top of a double boiler (we prefer the glass kind), heat the sugar, cream of tartar, egg whites, and water. Beat this mixture with an electric mixer until the frosting looks like well-beaten egg whites (about 5 to 7 minutes). Remove the top part of the double boiler from the heat and continue beating until the frosting stands in peaks. Now beat in the vanilla. Frost the cupcakes. Using store-bought icing in tubes in a variety of colors, write the number of the grade that the students are graduating into on the top of each cupcake

MAKES 9 CUPCAKES.

CARAMEL MINI POPCORN BALLS

24 squares vanilla caramel candies (7 to 8 ounces)

1 tablespoon water

5 to 6 cups popped popcorn

Place unwrapped caramel pieces and water in a large mixing bowl. Microwave on high for 1 minute. Stir. Continue microwaving on high, stirring every 30 seconds until the caramel is melted. Add the popcorn and toss until it is well coated. Wet your hands and shape the mixture into 2-inch balls. Wrap each popcorn ball in plastic wrap (colored wrap looks great).

MAKES 18 TO 20 BALLS.

GRAMPS THE GREATEST!

HORSERADISH MASHED POTATOES

8 pounds baking potatoes, peeled

3 teaspoons salt

½ cup heavy cream or milk, warm

¼ cup margarine, softened

1½ tablespoons white prepared horseradish

Salt and pepper to taste

Peel and quarter the potatoes. Place in cold water to keep them from browning. Drain. Place in a pot with water to cover and bring to a boil. Lower the heat and simmer, covered, for 20 minutes or until the potatoes are very soft and begin to fall apart. Remove from the heat and drain well. Beat the drained potatoes by hand (using an electric mixer or a food processor will result in gummy potatoes). Add the remaining ingredients and beat until fluffy and smooth. Add the horseradish slowly, ½ teaspoon at a time. Some people like more, others less. Taste before adding addition-

al horseradish. Serve immediately as is or with butter.

SERVES 14 TO 16.

CHICKEN VERA CRUZ

6 tablespoons butter or margarine

2 tablespoons oil

24 chicken parts (two per person)

1 teaspoon salt

½ teaspoon pepper

⅓ cup brandy (optional— it burns off)

4 cloves garlic, minced

¼ cup yellow chilies (canned), chopped

3 cans frozen orange juice

Chopped nuts

12 orange slices, rind removed

Melt the butter or margarine and the oil in a large, heavy skillet. Sauté the chicken pieces until golden brown on all sides. Season with salt and pepper. Pour the brandy over the chicken pieces and light to set aflame. The flames will die down quickly. Now add the chopped garlic and chilies. Blend in the undiluted orange juice and simmer, uncovered, for 25 minutes. Turn the pieces often so all sides are coated with the

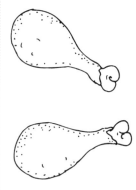

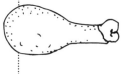

195

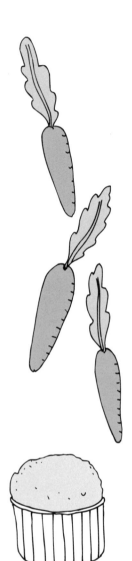

orange sauce. When the chicken is tender, remove to a heated plate and pour all the sauce over the chicken. Cover with the chopped nuts and garnish with the orange slices.

SERVES 12.

CARROT SOUFFLÉ

This is not your traditional soufflé. It is sweet and very easy to make and rises only a little.

1 pound carrots, peeled and cut into pieces

3 eggs

3 tablespoons flour

3 tablespoons sugar

1 teaspoon vanilla

½ cup (1 stick) butter or margarine, melted

dash of nutmeg

Preheat the oven to 350 degrees. Cook the carrots until very soft (even mushy). Blend them in the food processor with the eggs until very smooth. Add the rest of the ingredients. Pour into a 2-quart Pyrex or flat baking casserole. Bake for 40 minutes.

SERVES 4 TO 6.

JUST DESSERTS

¾ cup graham crackers

1 (13-ounce) can evaporated milk

¾ cup sugar

1 banana, mashed

Juice of 2 lemons

Crush graham crackers and spread evenly in 9-inch pie tin, reserving 1 tablespoon for a topping. Whip the milk until stiff peaks form and add remaining ingredients. Spread over graham cracker crumbs in the pan. Sprinkle reserved crumbs on top. Freeze.

SERVES 8.

HAVE A HEART

CRANBERRY PUNCH

Cranberry juice

Ginger ale

Lots of ice

The proportions are 2:1. Fill a heart-shaped cake pan with water. Freeze. The next day, combine cranberry juice and ginger ale in a punch bowl. When ready to serve, put the frozen heart into the punch bowl.

HEART SANDWICHES

- *1 (15½-ounce) can pink salmon, drained*
- *1 package (4 ounces) whipped cream cheese, or 1 (3-ounce) package regular cream cheese*
- *¼ teaspoon liquid hickory smoke*
- *2 tablespoons chopped chives*
- *1 tablespoon chopped parsley*
- *2 tablespoons fresh lemon juice*
- *Any bread cut into heart shapes with heart cookie cutter*

In a bowl, mix together all the ingredients but the bread. Cover and refrigerate overnight. In the morning, cut the crusts off the bread. Cut heart shapes with the cookie cutters. Toast lightly. Spread with enough salmon mixture to cover one heart. Cover with another heart bread.

STRAWBERRY DIVINE

Soften strawberry ice cream. Pack into a heart-shaped cake mold. Freeze. Unmold by dipping into hot water (do not cover the ice cream with water) for a count of 8, and inverting onto a serving dish.

COOKIE POPS

- *1 cup (2 sticks) butter or margarine*
- *¾ cup sugar*
- *1 egg, beaten*
- *1 teaspoon vanilla*
- *Red food coloring*
- *2¾ cups all-purpose flour*
- *1 teaspoon baking soda*
- *1 teaspoon cream of tartar*
- *Ice cream sticks*

In a food processor, mix together the butter and sugar until light in color. Add the egg and continue mixing. Add the vanilla and a couple of drops of the food coloring (you don't want a red cookie—just a pink one). Now add the flour, baking soda, and cream of tartar. The dough will form into a ball. Wrap the ball of dough in plastic and refrigerate for about 3 hours.

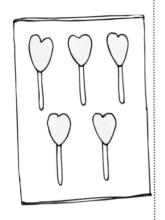

Preheat the oven to 350 degrees. On a floured cutting board, roll out the dough until about ¼ inch thick. Cut out with heart-shaped cookie cutters. Push one ice cream stick into each cookie. Bake for 10 to 12 minutes. When the cookies are cool, set aside. When the kids are at the party, let them decorate the cookies with pink frosting, red hots, sprinkles, etc.

HIT THE ROAD

SALAD BAR

Have one large bowl full of different kinds of lettuce (that's the one you put into the center of the tire). Surround that bowl with others full of salad fixings: chopped tomatoes, sliced cucumbers, chopped peppers, shredded carrots, sliced mushrooms, pine nuts, sliced onions.

In other containers, provide three different salad dressings. Since this is a large party, our dressing recipes call for two cups of dressing. You can keep any leftover dressing in the refrigerator.

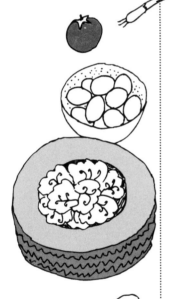

CLASSIC VINAIGRETTE

1 teaspoon Dijon mustard
1 garlic clove, sliced in half
½ teaspoon salt
¼ teaspoon ground pepper
¼ cup red wine vinegar
1 cup virgin olive oil

In a mixing bowl, combine the mustard, garlic, salt, and pepper. Add the vinegar and stir with a wire whisk until it is frothy. Slowly pour in the olive oil as you whisk constantly. The dressing will begin to thicken. Do not refrigerate—keep on the kitchen counter until ready to use.

BLUE CHEESE DRESSING

1 pound blue Cheese at room temperature
6 tablespoons heavy cream
4 tablespoons olive oil
Salt to taste
¼ teaspoon paprika
5 tablespoons lemon juice

Place the cheese in the food processor. Mix, using the chop start-and-stop method. Slowly add the cream and olive oil. Season with the salt and the paprika. Add the lemon juice and continue mixing. Chill in the refrigerator until ready to serve.

YOGURT AND HERB DRESSING

> 2 cups nonfat plain yogurt
>
> 4 tablespoons chopped fresh herbs (tarragon, basil, dill, parsley, chives)
>
> 1½ garlic cloves, finely chopped
>
> 2 teaspoons fresh lemon juice
>
> Fresh ground pepper, to taste

In the food processor, mix together the yogurt, chopped herbs, garlic, and lemon juice. Season to taste with the pepper. Refrigerate until you are ready to use (for about an hour or so) or the herbs will become very strong to the taste).

BREADS WITH SEASONED BUTTERS

Buy fresh breads the morning of the party. There are many varieties now available —try the seasoned breads like olive bread, rosemary bread, or pumpernickel with herb bread. Make some seasoned butters (these can also be served on plain sourdough or wheat breads to liven up their taste).

HERB BUTTER

> 1 cup butter or margarine, softened
>
> ½ cup mixed herbs (chopped parsley, thyme, rosemary, oregano, chives, etc.)
>
> ¼ teaspoon lemon juice

In the food processor, cream together the butter or margarine and the herbs. Add the lemon juice and continue creaming. You can season to taste with salt and pepper, if you like.

OLIVE BUTTER

> 1 cup pitted black Greek olives
>
> 1 cup butter or margarine, softened

Mix the two in the food processor until creamy smooth.

HONEY BUTTER

> 1 cup butter or margarine, softened
>
> 3 tablespoons honey

Mix the two in the food processor until creamy. Taste. If it is not sweet enough, add another tablespoon of honey.

BANANA SPLIT HEAVEN

Make your own banana splits: have a large container or three different kinds of ice cream. Cut bananas lengthwise (do this at the last minute so they won't turn brown). Have small bowls on the table, each full of maraschino cherries, hot fudge, whipped cream, crushed pineapple, nuts, sprinkles, and any other toppings you love.

THE JOKE'S ON YOU

SPAGHETTI PIE

6 ounces spaghetti

2 tablespoons butter

⅓ cup grated Parmesan cheese

2 eggs, well beaten

1 pound ground beef or pork sausage

½ cup chopped onion

¼ cup chopped green pepper

1 cup canned tomatoes, undrained and chopped

1 6-ounce can tomato paste

1 teaspoon sugar

1 teaspoon dried oregano

½ teaspoon garlic salt

1 cup cottage cheese

½ cup shredded mozzarella cheese

Cook the spaghetti according to the package instructions and drain. Stir in the butter, Parmesan cheese, and eggs. Form the spaghetti mixture into a crust in a buttered 10-inch pie plate. Preheat oven to 325 degrees.

Sauté the ground beef, onion, and pepper until the vegetables are tender and the meat is brown. Drain off the excess fat. Stir in the undrained tomatoes, tomato paste, sugar, oregano, and garlic salt. Heat through. Spread the cottage cheese over the bottom of the spaghetti crust. Fill the pie with the beef mixture. Sprinkle mozzarella cheese on the top. Bake for 5 minutes or longer, until the cheese melts.

SERVES 6–8 CHILDREN; MAKE TWO PIES FOR MORE KIDS OR IF YOUR KIDS ARE BIG EATERS.

AMBROSIA

12 oranges, peeled and sectioned

1 (16-ounce) can crushed pineapple

1 bag shredded coconut

1 cup orange juice

Mix all ingredients and moisten with orange juice. Refrigerate until it's time to serve.

CRAZY CUPCAKES

½ cup boiling water

½ cup cocoa powder

⅔ cup margarine, softened

1¾ cups sugar

1 teaspoon vanilla extract

2 eggs

1¼ cups all-purpose flour

1½ teaspoons baking soda

½ teaspoon salt

1⅓ cups buttermilk

1 recipe Chocolate Frosting (recipe follows)

1 bag gummy worms

Preheat the oven to 350 degrees. In a bowl, stir together the boiling water and cocoa until the cocoa has dissolved. In a food processor or with a mixer, cream the margarine, sugar, and vanilla until very smooth. Now add the eggs and beat again. In another bowl, mix together the flour, baking soda, and salt. Using two soup spoons, add the flour mixture and buttermilk alternately to the creamed mixture, one spoonful at a time. Now add the chocolate mixture and stir everything together. Pour the cake batter into prepared muffin tins lined with muffin papers. Bake for 20 minutes.

CHOCOLATE FROSTING

8 ounces semisweet baking chocolate or 1⅓ cups semisweet chocolate chips

½ cup whipping cream

1 cup sugar

In a small pan, combine the chocolate, cream, and sugar. Cook over low heat until the chocolate is melted and smooth. Stir constantly! Make sure the mixture doesn't boil. It's ready when it is thick and smooth (12 to 15 minutes).

When the cupcakes are frosted, make a hole in each at the center of the top and add 2 or 3 gummy worms coming out of the cupcake.

★ *You might want to get your guests' attention by adding extra spices to one of your dishes.*

★ *Freeze large plastic spiders in ice cubes and put them in the punch.*

★ *Roast marshmallows over the fire.*

★ *You may throw out the bay leaf, save the vegetables, and purée them in a food processor. Add them to the soup another day to make a cream of chicken vegetable soup.*

LOOK, IT'S SNOWING!

SNOW CONES

Make snow cones outside out of shaved ice with 2 tablespoons of your favorite juice. Serve in a paper cup.

TRIPLE CHICKEN NOODLE SOUP

1 whole large chicken, giblets removed
1 onion, quartered
2 carrots, peeled and halved
2 stalks celery, washed
1 bay leaf
1 tablespoon salt
¼ teaspoon pepper
¼ cup fresh parsley sprigs
3 garlic cloves, halved
1 pound egg noodles, macaroni, or alphabet pasta

Place the chicken in the center of a large stockpot and cover with cold water (3 quarts should do it). Bring to a boil, reduce the heat, and simmer until just about tender, about 1½ hours. Add the onion, carrots, celery, bay leaf, salt, pepper, parsley, and garlic. Cook for about 1 hour. Remove the chicken and all the vegetables. Strain the broth. Add 1 pound of egg noodles, macaroni, or alphabet noodles and cook for 20 minutes.

MAKES ABOUT 3 QUARTS.

SNOWBALLS

Put a scoop of ice cream on a piece of waxed paper covered with coconut. Roll the ice cream in the coconut and put in the freezer. Work fast. Keep the bowl in the freezer. When you take the snowballs out, let them sit for a minute or two and they'll separate.

MASK-ERADE

CHURASSCO

¼ cup fresh lemon juice
¼ teaspoon salt
¼ teaspoon pepper
1 garlic clove
1 teaspoon Dijon mustard
1 tablespoon olive oil
2 pounds beef, lamb or chicken, cut into chunks

Mix the lemon juice, salt, pepper, garlic, mustard, and oil in a bowl and marinate the beef, refrigerated, for at least 5 hours. Skewer marinated chunks on sticks and grill for 5 minutes on each side. You can cook them under the broiler as well.

COUSCOUS

1 tablespoon virgin olive oil
½ large white onion, chopped
1 garlic clove, chopped
1 cup chicken broth
2 tablespoons butter or margarine
Pinch of salt
1 cup dry couscous
salt to taste

In a small frying pan, heat the olive oil and sauté the chopped onions over low heat until golden. Add the garlic and sauté another 2 minutes. Set aside.

In a saucepan, combine the chicken broth, butter, and a pinch of salt and bring to a boil. Remove from the heat. Add the couscous and stir well. Add the sautéed onions and let stand for about 5 minutes. Fluff with a fork.

MAKES ABOUT 5 SERVINGS.

TOMATO SALAD

4 tomatoes
1 tablespoon olive oil
½ teaspoon fresh lemon juice or herb vinegar
1 tablespoon fresh basil, chopped
Salt and pepper to taste

Dice the tomatoes. Add the other ingredients and serve.

CHOCOLATE BANANAS

6 bananas, peeled
12 wooden ice cream bar sticks
12 ounces chocolate chips
½ cup hot water

Cut the bananas in half crosswise. Insert a wooden stick in the cut end of each banana. Place the bananas on a piece of wax paper and freeze them for 1 hour. Meanwhile, melt the chocolate chips in the hot water. Dip the frozen bananas in the chocolate so that they are covered. Let chocolate set, wrap bananas in aluminum foil, and return to freezer until you're ready to serve.

MAKES 12 SERVINGS.

203

PLAY BALL

CARAMEL CORN

2 cups brown sugar
½ cup white corn syrup
1 cup (2 sticks) margarine
½ teaspoon salt
6 to 8 quarts popped popcorn (1½ to 2 cups unpopped popcorn)

Put brown sugar, corn syrup, margarine, and salt into a pan and bring to a boil. Boil 5 minutes and pour over popcorn. Stir well. Put into 2 large pans and bake in 250-degree oven for 1 hour. Stir every 15 minutes. Make into balls.

MAKES 2–3 DOZEN BALLS DEPENDING ON THEIR SIZE.

HOT DOGS ON A STICK

Insert a wooden skewer into raw hot dog. Grill hot dogs on a hot grill for about 10 minutes. Serve with various accompaniments (relish, mustard, grilled or chopped onions, etc.).

MICROWAVE CORN ON THE COB

For each ear of corn; pull down one side of the husk and remove as much of the silk as you can. Replace the husk. To microwave, simply place two at a time in the oven for 1 minute on one side at high heat, then turn over for an additional minute.

AUTOGRAPH CAKE

This is a delicious sheet cake with buttercream frosting. When the cake is done, hand out individual frosting tubes in different colors. Have each guest autograph the cake with his or her name.

1¼ cups sugar
1 (8-ounce) package cream cheese, softened
1½ cups butter or margarine, softened
2¼ cups cake flour (not self-rising)
2 teaspoons baking powder
4 eggs
1¼ teaspoons vanilla extract

Preheat the oven to 350 degrees. Grease and flour a 13x9-inch baking pan.

Place the sugar, cream cheese, and 1 cup of the butter into a mixing bowl. With the electric mixer at low speed, beat together until light and fluffy. Add the flour, baking powder, eggs, and vanilla. Continue beating at low speed until everything is blended. Scrape the bowl and blend again. Increase the speed to medium and beat another 2 minutes.

Pour the batter into the prepared baking pan. Bake for 25 to 30 minutes or until a toothpick inserted into the middle comes out clean. Cool for about 10 minutes.

BUTTERCREAM FROSTING

4 cups powdered sugar

6 tablespoons butter or margarine, softened

3 to 4 tablespoons milk

1½ teaspoons vanilla

½ teaspoon salt

In a large bowl with a mixer at medium speed (or in a food processor fitted with the metal blade), beat all the ingredients until very smooth, adding more milk if necessary to make a good spreading consistency. Frost the cake. When done, hand out those individual frosting tubes and let everyone put their autograph on the cake.

SHAKE, RATTLE, AND ROLL

SHAKE-AND-QUAKE CHICKEN

Two 2½-pound chickens, quartered

½ cup olive oil

1 lemon

Salt and pepper to taste

Buy the chicken cut into quarters. Rub the chicken pieces with olive oil and lemon juice. Start the fire in the barbecue grill, and when the coals are glowing, broil the chicken pieces 5 or 6 inches from the heat. Turn after 8 to 10 minutes. Total cooking time should be 25 to 30 minutes, depending on the intensity of the heat. Salt and pepper to taste.

MAKES ENOUGH FOR 8 ADULTS OR 10 TO 12 CHILDREN.

JELL-O JIGGLES

2 (3-ounce) packages Jell-O strawberry gelatin

2 cups boiling water or fruit juice

1 cup sliced strawberries

Dissolve the gelatin in boiling water. Add 1½ cups water or fruit juice to the gelatin and

★ *You can also buy Shake 'n' Bake chicken mix, the kind you place in a paper bag and shake so bread crumbs or crushed corn flakes stick to the chicken. Remember to let the kids do the shaking—it's their favorite part.*

pour 1 cup into an 8-inch layer pan. Chill until set but not firm. Arrange the sliced strawberries on the gelatin—you can make an abstract design or a funny face. Chill again until set, and pour on the remaining gelatin. Chill until the whole dessert is firm, about three hours. When done, unmold on a large platter. If you have created a face, it will jiggle.

MAKES ABOUT 8 SERVINGS.

FAULTY FRIES

8 baking potatoes
¼ cup vegetable oil
Salt to taste

Peel the potatoes and cut into sticks, approximately ¼ inch by 3 inches. Coat with vegetable oil and bake on a large cookie sheet at 400 degrees for about 40 minutes or until golden brown. Salt to taste.

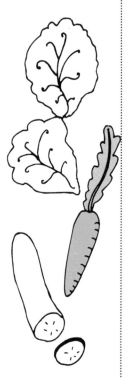

SEISMIC SALAD

Combine several different lettuces, diced carrots, peppers, cucumbers, and tomatoes. "Shake them up" and then add oil and vinegar for the dressing.

BUMP-ALONG BROWNIES

½ cup butter
2 (1-ounce) squares of unsweetened chocolate
1 cup sugar
⅔ cup self-rising flour
1 teaspoon vanilla
2 eggs
¾ cup chopped pecans
4 ounces chocolate chips (half a bag)

Preheat the oven to 350 degrees. Grease the bottom of an 8-inch square pan. Melt the butter and chocolate in a saucepan, then remove from heat. Add the sugar, flour, and vanilla. Stir to mix. Add the eggs and beat well. Stir in the pecans and chocolate chips. Bake about 30 minutes. Cut into squares.

MAKES ABOUT 8 BROWNIES.

SIMPLY SUMMER

GRILLED SUMMER SPARE RIBS

> *Rack of pork ribs, trimmed of fat, or 4 or 5 per person*
> *Barbecue sauce (recipe follows)*

Bake the ribs in a roasting pan at 400 degrees for 30 minutes. Pour off the fat. Then place the ribs on the grill. Baste every 10 minutes or so with the barbecue sauce (the ribs need basting when the sauce looks dry) until done. Turn and continue to baste.

BARBECUE SAUCE

> *1 cup (2 sticks) butter or margarine*
> *2½ cups water*
> *¼ cup vinegar*
> *¼ cup chopped onion*
> *2 garlic cloves, chopped*
> *1 teaspoon sugar*
> *1 teaspoon paprika*
> *2 teaspoons salt*
> *2 teaspoons chili powder*
> *2 teaspoons black pepper*
> *¼ tablespoon Tabasco*
> *1 teaspoon dry mustard*

Bring all the ingredients to a boil. Reduce the heat and simmer for half an hour. Use for basting the ribs.

CORN ON THE GRILL

> *1 ear of corn per person*

One section at a time, carefully peel back the husk of each ear of corn. Pull off all the thread-like fibers and return the husk sections to the original position. (If you like, you can tie the tips of the husk to the corn with a piece of string.) Soak in water for about 10 minutes. Drain, but don't dry. Lay the ears of corn on an oiled grill rack above medium coals. Grill, turning the ears often until the husks are a deep brown, for about 15 minutes. Remove the corn with tongs, peel back the husks, and butter the corn. Put the husks back to melt the butter and keep the corn warm. Serve with the husks on (each guest can peel back the husks and remove them).

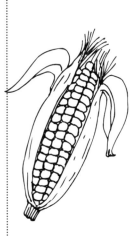

207

★ *Marc Gilbar loves Thai food. He has created a sauce that he dips his barbecued ribs into after they are cooked. He says the combination of the barbecue and the Thai flavors is exceptional. Here's how to make his Thai dipping sauce:*

⅓ cup sugar

2 tablespoons cornstarch

⅓ cup soy sauce

3 tablespoons vinegar

¾ teaspoon crushed
   red pepper

In a small saucepan, combine the sugar and cornstarch. Mix with a wooden spoon. Add the soy sauce, vinegar, and red pepper. Stirring constantly, cook until the sauce thickens. Set aside until it cools and then dip the ribs into the sauce.

SUMMER GREEN SALAD

Lettuce of any kind (try mixing several different sorts)

With this meal, we like a simple green salad with a light lemon vinaigrette dressing.

LEMON VINAIGRETTE DRESSING

1 garlic clove, cut in half

1 teaspoon Dijon mustard

2 leaves fresh basil, chopped

2 tablespoons fresh lemon juice

1 cup virgin olive oil

Salt and pepper to taste

In a small bowl, place the garlic, mustard, basil, and lemon juice. Whisk. Gradually add the olive oil, whisking constantly, until the vinaigrette is frothy. Add salt and pepper to taste.

BAKED BEANS

½ pound sliced bacon, diced

2 medium-sized onions, chopped

2 (1-pound, 4-ounce) cans pork and beans or vegetarian beans

1½ teaspoons dry mustard

1 (9-ounce) can crushed pineapple

¼ cup chili sauce

¼ teaspoon salt

Sauté bacon and onions slowly until onions are soft. Drain off fat. Combine bacon and onions with beans, mustard, pineapple, chili sauce, and salt, and put into a casserole or bean pot (about 1½-quart size). Cover and bake in a very slow oven, 275 degrees, for 1½ to 2 hours.

MAKES 6 SERVINGS.

CLASSIC BROWNIES

3 squares unsweetened chocolate

½ cup (1 stick) butter

1 cup sugar

2 large eggs

¾ cup sifted flour

¼ teaspoon baking powder

¾ cup chopped pecans

Preheat oven to 350 degrees. Melt the chocolate in a double boiler over barely simmering water. Add a little of the butter. Meanwhile, cream the remaining butter and the sugar in a bowl until well blended. Beat the eggs into the sugar-butter mixture, then add the flour and baking powder by thirds. Fold in the melted chocolate and nuts and pour the batter into an oiled 8-inch square pan. Bake 30 to 35 minutes, or until the top is lightly crusty and the sides start to pull away from the pan. Cool and cut into squares.

MAKES 12 BROWNIES.

SPRING FLING

MAYPOLE COOKIES

- *⅓ cup butter*
- *½ cup tightly packed brown sugar*
- *1 egg*
- *¼ cup currants*
- *1 teaspoon grated lemon zest*
- *1 cup flour*
- *1 teaspoon baking powder*

Preheat the oven to 350 degrees. In a food processor fitted with the steel blade, mix the butter until it is lemon-colored. Gradually add the brown sugar, a scoop at a time, while the processor is on. Add the egg and blend again. Pour the batter out of the processor into a bowl, add the currants and lemon zest, and mix with a wooden spoon.

In another bowl, sift the flour and baking powder. Add the currant mixture to the flour and mix well. Grease a cookie sheet. Drop the cookie dough by rounded tablespoonfuls 2 inches apart and bake in the center of the oven for about 10 minutes, or until lightly brown.

MAKES ABOUT 24 COOKIES.

CHOCOLATE MINT COOKIES

- *6 ounces chocolate chips*
- *1 cup flour*
- *½ teaspoon baking soda*
- *½ cup margarine or butter*
- *¼ teaspoon vanilla*
- *½ cup sugar*
- *1 egg*
- *1 teaspoon mint extract*
- *2 tablespoons water*

Preheat the oven to 350 degrees. Melt ½ cup of the chocolate chips in a glass pot or a double boiler. Let cool. Sift together the flour and baking soda. In the food processor, using the steel blade, blend the butter, vanilla, sugar, and egg until the mixture is smooth. Add the flour mixture. Now add the melted chocolate, mint extract, and water. Mix again until creamy and smooth. Take out of the processor and place in a bowl. Add the rest of the chocolate chips and mix carefully with a wooden spoon. You now have a chocolate chip mint cookie dough.

Grease two cookie sheets. Drop the cookie dough by rounded tablespoonfuls 2 to 3 inches apart. Bake for 10 to 12 minutes. Let cool. Refrigerate and serve the next day.

MAKES 24 COOKIES.

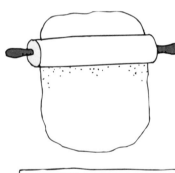

LETTER COOKIES

    4½ cups sifted flour
    4 teaspoons baking powder
    1 teaspoon salt
    1 cup (2 sticks)
        unsalted butter, softened
    2 cups sugar
    2 eggs
    ½ cup milk
    ½ teaspoon vanilla extract

Preheat the oven to 375 degrees. Grease two baking sheets. Sift together the dry ingredients. In a large bowl, cream the butter and sugar until fluffy. Add the eggs one at a time, beating well after each addition. Add the dry ingredients 1 cup at a time,

alternating with the milk and vanilla, beating well after each addition. Wrap and chill for at least 1 hour. Divide the dough into 4 pieces. Roll 1 piece at a time on a floured board and cut into shapes of letters. Bake for 8 to 10 minutes. Cool for a minute or so on the baking sheet, then remove to a wire rack and let cool completely.

MAKES APPROXIMATELY 40 3-INCH COOKIES.

ORANGE COOKIES

    2½ cups sifted flour
    ¼ teaspoon salt
    ¼ teaspoon baking soda
    1 cup vegetable shortening
    ½ cup sugar
    ½ cup brown sugar
    1 egg, beaten
    2 tablespoons frozen orange
        juice
    1 teaspoon orange zest

Preheat the oven to 400 degrees. In a mixing bowl, sift the flour with the salt and baking soda. In a food processor with the steel blade, mix together the shortening, sugars, egg, orange juice, and zest until smooth. Add the flour mixture gradually while still processing.

Grease two cookie sheets. Drop the cookie dough by rounded tablespoonfuls 2 inches apart. Bake about 12 minutes until golden brown.
MAKES 24 TO 30 COOKIES.

TRIFLE

1 pound macaroons

2 cups cranberry juice (made from concentrate using half the amount of water to make it stronger)

30 to 40 ladyfingers

½ cup sugar

2 tablespoons flour

1 egg, beaten

2 cups hot milk

½ pound almonds, chopped

½ pound candied cherries, halved

4 cups heavy cream, whipped

2 cups strawberry or raspberry jam

Soak the macaroons in the cranberry juice. Line a large glass bowl with the ladyfinger halves. Mix the sugar and flour with the egg, gradually adding the hot milk. Cook in a double boiler until it is thick to form a custard; be sure to stir it constantly. Cool. Now add the almonds and cherries and 3 cups of the whipped cream. Pour the custard mixture over the ladyfingers and top with the soaked macaroons. Alternately (you will have a striped effect), cover with some more ladyfingers, strawberry jam, and the rest of the whipped cream.

FLOWERPOTS

Small clay pots

Assorted ice cream

Oreo or plain chocolate cookies, crumbled

Green candies

To make these little flowerpots, simple fill each clay pot with alternate layers of soft ice cream (chocolate or mint) and crumbled cookies, and top with any green candies. Stick real flowers (those with wide, thick stems stand up best) into the top and through the ice cream, and freeze. When done, stick real daisies or plastic ones in the center of each pot.

★ *Be sure the flowers you use are nontoxic and pesticide-free. Check with your local garden center if you have any questions.*

MAY PARFAITS

*1 (3-ounce) package straw-
  berry Jell-O mix*
1 cup boiling water
¾ cup cold water
*2 tablespoons strawberry
  preserves*
½ cup whipped cream

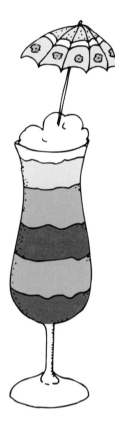

Dissolve the Jell-O in the boiling water; measure ¼ cup and set aside. Add the cold water to the remaining Jell-O and chill until thickened. Meanwhile, add the preserves to the ¼ cup Jell-O that you set aside. Chill until slightly thickened and then fold into the whipped cream. Into clear stem glasses, alternately pour the clear Jell-O and the creamy mixture (this recipe will fill four glasses). When done, top with a miniature paper umbrella.

LEMON FIZZY

8 ounces lemon-lime soda
*1 scoop lemon or lime
  sherbet*

Place a scoop of the sherbet in the bottom of a tall glass. Pour soda over it. Finish off with a straw. Serve immediately.

MAKES 1 SERVING.

STAMPEDE

SALSA AND CHIPS

*1 small red pepper, seeded
  and chopped*
*1 small yellow pepper,
  seeded and chopped*
1 medium onion, chopped
4 green onions, chopped
*3 plum tomatoes, seeded
  and chopped*
2 tablespoons olive oil
*1 (8-ounce) can tomato
  sauce or 1 (8-ounce) bottle chili sauce*
3 tablespoons cilantro
1 teaspoon black pepper

In a skillet, sauté peppers, onions, and tomatoes in oil until tender, about 4 minutes. Add the tomato sauce or chili sauce and cilantro and cook for 6 minutes. Add the black pepper and a dash of salt, if needed.

TAMALE PIE

1½ pounds ground beef

1 (28-ounce) can whole tomatoes

1 (8½-ounce) can creamed corn

1 large and 1 small onion, chopped

1 teaspoon chili powder

1 large garlic clove, minced

Salt and pepper to taste

1 cup yellow cornmeal

1 can pitted black olives

Cheddar cheese

Preheat the oven to 350 degrees. Brown beef in large pot. Add the tomatoes, corn, onion, chili powder, garlic, and salt and pepper. When all is mixed, add cornmeal and olives. Cook about 15 minutes. Put in large casserole. Grate cheddar cheese onto the top. Place in oven for about 30 minutes.

SERVES 10.

STIRRUP

A glass of milk, a drop of vanilla, and a teaspoon of chocolate syrup. You've got to "stirrup" to drink it down!

MUD PIE

1 pound Oreo cookies, crushed

½ cup (1 stick) butter, melted

2 pints ice cream, any flavor, softened

Mix Oreo crumbs with melted butter and press into two pans. Fill with ice cream. Freeze until firm.

FUDGE SAUCE

Combine 2 tablespoons of butter with 10 1-ounce cubes of semi-sweet chocolate. Heat in a double boiler. Pour over the mud pie.

TIME-TRAVELING BIRTHDAY

PIZZA CLOCKS

1 baby Boboli shell

¼ cup tomato sauce

¼ cup shredded mozzarella cheese

Black olives, sliced

Bell peppers, sliced

Mushrooms, sliced

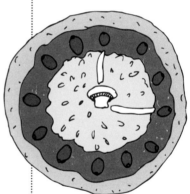

Preheat the oven to 450 degrees. Place the pizza shell on a pan. Spread the tomato sauce on the shell and sprinkle cheese on top. Using black olives as numbers, mushroom as the center and 2 bell pepper slices as hands, make a clock (see drawing on page 213). Heat in the oven according to package instructions until the cheese melts. Serve.

MAKES 1.

SALAD BAR

Leaves of 1 head lettuce and a selection of mushrooms, carrots, celery, olives, tomatoes, and cucumber, washed and sliced.

Put all ingredients into individual bowls. Allow guests to serve themselves at this do-it-yourself salad bar. Don't forget a selection of dressings. See pages 198–199 for some of our favorites.

SUNDAE BAR

Make your own sundae bar. Serve each guest a bowl with a scoop of chocolate and a scoop of vanilla ice cream. In individual serving bowls with spoons, provide a selection of whipped cream, maraschino cherries, crushed pineapple, walnuts, sprinkles, banana slices, chocolate sauce, caramel sauce—whatever you like to make a super sundae bar.

FORTUNE CUPCAKES

⅓ cup shortening
2 cups sifted cake flour (not self-rising)
1 cup sugar
2½ teaspoons baking powder
¾ teaspoon salt
1 slightly beaten egg
¾ cup milk
1 teaspoon vanilla

Preheat the oven to 375 degrees. Stir the shortening to soften. Sift in the dry ingredients. Add the egg and half the milk. Mix until the flour is moist. Beat for 2 minutes at low speed with an electric mixer or in the food processor. Add the remaining milk and vanilla; beat 1 minute longer. Place paper baking cups in muffin pans; fill ½ full. On small pieces of paper, write a fortune, a joke, or a message and fold them. Place one message in the center of each batter-filled baking cup.

Bake for about 20 minutes or until a toothpick comes out clean.

MAKES 20.

UNDER THE HARVEST MOON

CORN SOUP

6 ears corn

4 tablespoons margarine

Salt and pepper to taste

3 cups chicken broth

4 to 6 tablespoons heavy cream (optional)

Scrape the ears of corn. This will give you nearly 4 cups of corn kernels. In a saucepan, melt the margarine. Add the corn and salt and pepper to taste. Cook for about 3 minutes. Add the chicken broth and simmer, stirring, for 15 minutes. When cool, pour into the food processor and process until smooth. If you like, you can press the soup through a sieve; otherwise, place back into the saucepan and warm. Add cream if you like.

OLD-FASHIONED CHICKEN POT PIE

8 to 10 pieces of chicken, skinned (breasts, thighs, and legs)

1 onion, peeled and cut into quarters

2 stalks celery

6 carrots, peeled and sliced

1 box frozen peas, thawed

2 cups mushrooms, cleaned and sliced

4 tablespoons margarine

Salt and pepper to taste

2 tablespoons flour

Frozen biscuit dough

In a large pot, place the chicken pieces, onion, celery, and half the carrots. Cover with water and bring to a boil. Simmer about 45 minutes, or until the chicken is soft. Remove from heat and let the pot cool.

Preheat the oven to 450 degrees. Strain the soup, throwing away the vegetables, but keeping the chicken broth and the chicken pieces. (You should have 2 cups of chicken broth. If you have less, add a little more water, or water with a chicken bouillon cube dissolved in it.) Bone the chicken and chop the meat.

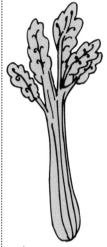

★ *Annie's mom adds freshly popped popcorn to the soup just when it is served. Kids love this!*

In a saucepan, melt 2 tablespoons margarine and add the remaining carrots, the peas, and the mushrooms. Brown lightly. Season with salt and pepper. Set aside. In another saucepan, melt the remaining butter and add the flour. Whisk. Add the 2 cups of chicken soup and whisk again. Bring to a boil and cook until thick. Taste to see whether you need to season with salt and pepper. Now add the chicken and the vegetable mixture. Pour everything into a round 8-inch soufflé dish. Cover the dish with ready-made biscuit dough. Prick with a fork. Bake until the crust is a golden brown, usually 10 to 12 minutes.

SERVES 10 TO 12.

CORNBREAD MUFFINS

1 cup stone-ground corn-meal

1 cup flour

⅓ cup sugar

2½ teaspoons baking powder

½ teaspoon baking soda

¼ teaspoon salt

1 cup buttermilk

¾ pound bacon, fried and crumbled

6 tablespoons margarine, melted

1 egg, slightly beaten

Preheat the oven to 400 degrees. Combine the cornmeal, flour, sugar, baking powder, baking soda, and salt in a mixing bowl. Stir in the buttermilk, bacon, margarine, and egg. Mix with a wooden spoon until just blended (not too much). Pour into a greased 12-cup muffin tin. Bake for 25 minutes.

PUMPKIN WITH BAKED APPLES AND ICE CREAM

1 medium pumpkin

Vegetable oil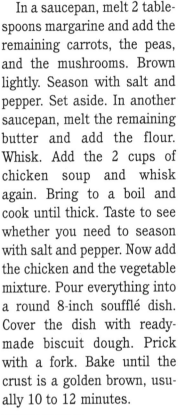

Maple syrup

6 small red apples, washed, dried, and cored

Vanilla ice cream

Preheat the oven to 350 degrees. Line a cookie sheet with aluminum foil. Wash the pumpkin in cold water and pat dry. Cut a circle approximately 4 inches in diameter around the stem. Lift the stem and put the top aside. Scoop out the seeds and soft pulp. Brush the inside of the pumpkin with vegetable oil. (Reserve the seeds for cleaning and roasting later.) Spoon 1 teaspoon of maple syrup into each apple. Place the apples upright inside the pumpkin. Spoon 2 teaspoons

of maple syrup over all. Replace the pumpkin top.

Put the pumpkin on the cookie sheet and place it in the oven. Bake until the pumpkin and the apples are tender, about 1½ to 2 hours. Remove the pumpkin from the oven. Remove the top carefully because it will be very hot. Remove the apples. Slice the pumpkin into 6 pieces. Put a slice of pumpkin and an apple on each plate, and top with a scoop of ice cream.

MULLED CIDER

6 1-inch cinnamon sticks

1 tablespoon whole cloves

1 tablespoon whole allspice

2 pieces whole nutmeg

2 whole lemons, cut in halves

2 cups brown sugar

1 gallon apple cider

16 whole cinnamon sticks

Tie the first four ingredients in a cloth bag. In a large pot, place the lemons, sugar, and cider, and stir together. Add the spice bag. Bring to a boil and simmer for 30 to 45 minutes. Remove the bag and serve hot with a whole cinnamon stick in each mug.

SALAD

Leaves of 1 head red leaf lettuce, well washed and dried

Leaves of 1 head romaine, well washed and dried

Leaves of 1 head curly endive, well washed and dried

Toss the leaves together with the vinaigrette and serve.

VINAIGRETTE

1 garlic clove, peeled and pierced

2 tablespoons herb vinegar

⅔ cup virgin olive oil (flavored olive oil is also great)

Pinches of herbs: tarragon, basil, oregano

½ teaspoon Dijon mustard

Place the garlic in a glass bowl and add the vinegar. Slowly pour the olive oil into the bowl, whisking all the time. Add the herbs and continue whisking. Now add the mustard, still whisking. Remove the garlic.

WELCOME HOME, BABY!

BREAKFAST

MELON BALLS

Cut cantaloupe in half. Remove the seeds and throw them away. Use round melon ball scoop (or small spoon, if that's all that is available) to scoop out pieces of melon. Pile in a bowl. Top with plain yogurt.

CINNAMON TOAST

Butter, softened
8 slices white bread
4 rounded tablespoons sugar
½ teaspoon ground cinnamon

Spread butter generously on the bread slices and place them on a cookie sheet. Combine the sugar and the cinnamon. Sprinkle a scant tablespoon of the cinnamon sugar on each slice. Place the bread in the oven 6 to 8 inches from the broiler. Broil until the cinnamon sugar is bubbly, but remove before the crusts are brown. Cool, then cut into triangles and serve with hot tea. SERVES 8.

LUNCH

PEANUT BUTTER AND BANANA SANDWICHES

Peanut butter (chunky or smooth)
2 pieces bread per person
½ banana per person

Spread the peanut butter on one side of the bread. Cut the banana into coin shapes and place on top of the peanut butter. Cover with another slice of bread and cut in half.

STRAWBERRY FLIP

1 cup diced strawberries (fresh or frozen)
1 cup milk
8 to 10 ice cubes
1 tablespoon sugar

Clean and cut up the strawberries. Put all the ingredients in a blender and mix for 30 seconds. Makes 2 servings.

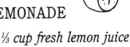

LEMONADE

⅓ cup fresh lemon juice
¼ cup sugar
1 quart cold water
Ice cubes

Put the lemon juice in a tall pitcher. Add 1 cup of water and the sugar. Stir until the sugar is dissolved. Add the rest of the water and stir. Taste. Add the ice cubes.

MAKES 1 PITCHER.

DINNER

TACOS

Package of preshaped taco shells

1 pound ground beef

4 ounces cheddar cheese, enough to make 1 cup grated cheese

1 tomato

1 bunch green onions

1 head iceberg lettuce

½ teaspoon salt

¼ teaspoon pepper

Hot sauce

Brown the ground beef in a frying pan over medium heat. Stir often, breaking the meat up into small pieces. It is done when it loses its red color. Drain off the fat and put the meat into a bowl. Warm the taco shells according to the package directions. Grate the cheese. Place in a bowl. Cut the tomato in wedges, chop the green onions, and shred the lettuce. Place all in individual bowls. Everyone assembles according to individual taste.

CHILLY CHOCOLATE PIE

1 (3.4-ounce) package chocolate pudding

9-inch pie shell

1 can whipped cream

Make the pudding according to the package instructions and let it cool. Bake the pie shell. Pour the pudding into the shell and refrigerate. Decorate with whipped cream.

SERVES 8.

219

INDEX